Burning Bright

i

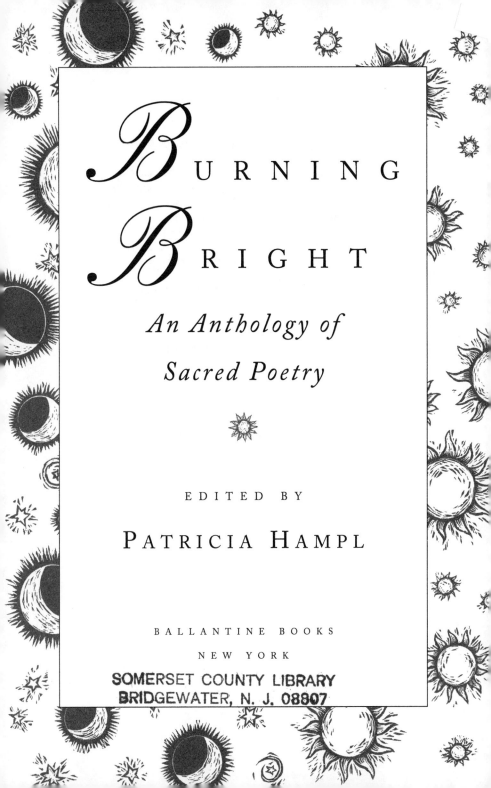

BURNING

BRIGHT

An Anthology of
Sacred Poetry

EDITED BY

PATRICIA HAMPL

BALLANTINE BOOKS

NEW YORK

Permission acknowledgments appear on pages 175–178,
which constitute an extension of the copyright page.

Library of Congress Cataloging-in-Publication Data
Burning Bright : an anthology of sacred poetry / edited by Patricia Hampl.—1st ed.
p.   cm.
ISBN 0-345-38029-0
1. Religious poetry.   2. Day—Poetry.   I. Hampl, Patricia, 1946–.
PN6110.R4B85   1995   95-8900
808.81'9382—dc20   CIP

Text design by Mary A. Wirth

Manufactured in the United States of America
First Edition: November 1995
10 9 8 7 6 5 4 3 2 1

God, the Lord God, has spoken
and summoned the world
from the rising of the sun
to its setting. . . .

—PSALM 50

$\mathcal{C}$ONTENTS

$\mathscr{I}$NTRODUCTION

This is a reader's anthology, not a scholar's, and is meant to be a companion for the day. In this spirit, it belongs to the tradition of pagan and sacred collections that precede even the printed book. The Christian "Book of Hours" is only the best known of these kinds of day books which attempt to make the day holy—or at least bearable. The West's polytheistic classical world also encouraged a personal anthology of beloved writings known as the *silva rerum*—a forest of things. While not linked to liturgical use as the "Book of Hours" was, the *silva rerum* honored the human impulse to surround (and penetrate) a life with sustaining and inspiring writing.

The poems in this forest of writings are divided into three sections—not according to religion or historical period (those are purposely mixed together as a way of honoring the kinship of the three great religions—Judaism, Christianity, and Islam). Rather, in the spirit of Western prayer disciplines, the organization is shaped according to time of day: Morning, Noon, and Night.

Defining the day into a cycle of prayer is a discipline common to all three traditions of Western monotheism. In fact, the need to distinguish time—hour, day, season—lies deep within the instinct to pray, as it does within consciousness itself. The enduring monastic tradition in Christianity, for instance, is based not on the Eucharist or the Sacraments, but on the Divine Office, which is a great wheel of cyclical prayers running from morning through night. The Book of Hours was designed to follow the Office.

This preoccupation with time and the need to *mark* it is the impulse behind the first creative act of the monotheistic imagination: the distinction of light from dark:

God said, "Let there be light," and there was light. God saw
that light was good, and God divided light from darkness.
God called light "day," and darkness he called "night."
Evening came and morning came: the first day.

Even before that ("In the beginning"), God created heaven and earth. But that creative attempt was not, apparently, an entirely successful project, for the author of Genesis remarks immediately after the creation of heaven and earth, "The earth was a formless void." The creation of earth does not occasion the positive response that follows the separation of light from dark: "God saw that light was good." The acknowledgment of the goodness of this creative act, this first distinction of "the void," is also the first gesture toward marking time. It is the first "good news" in Scripture.

One of the hallmarks of religion is its attempt to claim time in order to sacralize it. In the realm of the spirit—especially the monotheistic spirit—time is more essential than place. When the muezzin calls out morning and evening across a Muslim city, when the Angelus bells ring across a Christian village, it is time, not location, not even God, which is being sanctified. This clock-watching sensibility lies at the heart of the Psalms, the oldest and most cherished poetry of Western monotheism. Many of these ancient Jewish poems have seasonal and daily subtitles or directives as ancient as their texts: Psalm 3, for instance, is a "Morning prayer of the upright"; Psalm 134 is "for the evening liturgy."

The poems in this collection do not include the Psalms or any poetry from any version of the Bible or the Koran. Even the non-scriptural "Anonymous" of so many early Christian lyrics is absent. The poems here were written over centuries, but each one is ascribed to an identifiable person, a poet who was conscious of writing a poem. Some of the poets are identifiably "religious." Most are not. Rumi, one of the greatest, barely admitted he was a poet, in spite of his astonishing output: well over thirty thousand poems, and yet he once remarked, dismissively:

> I am affectionate to such a degree that when these friends come to me, for fear that they may be wearied I speak poetry so they may be occupied with that. Otherwise, what have I to do with poetry? By Allah, I care nothing for poetry, and there is nothing worse in my eyes than that. It has become incumbent upon me, as when a man plunges his hands into tripe and washes it out for the sake of a guest's appetite, because the guest's appetite is for tripe.

In choosing poems, I tried to represent the *search* for the sacred which even (I've come to think, especially) drives contemporary poets. Even in a culture as apparently secular as ours, this search is profound. We may not always know what we believe, but we know what we long for. Longing in the face of uncertainty is what distinguishes the modern spiritual quest. It is precisely the tension between the impulse toward mystery and the wariness of our secular mentality which generates the most passionate spiritual poetry, at least to my contemporary ear.

Sixty-seven poets are represented in the anthology—some by multiple poems. Emily Dickinson, Rainer Maria Rilke, Yehuda Amichai, Nelly Sachs, and Rumi (to name a few) are obvious repeaters. Of the anthology's population of sixty-seven poets, sixteen are Jewish and sixteen Islamic. Of the remaining thirty-five, it wouldn't be exact to say all are Christian. Many don't quite fit under that label. To name only a few obvious exceptions, Wallace Stevens certainly wouldn't be sitting in the same pew with Gerard Manley Hopkins, and Emily Dickinson's aloofness from Christianity is the subject of much of her work. Thomas Merton, a Cistercian monk and celebrated memoirist and spiritual writer, is represented here by his version of a poem by a Chinese Zen sage. And Allen Ginsberg, whose elegy for his mother, *Kaddish*, is one of the great poems of the age, is here with poems about his Buddhist meditation practice, rather than his Jewish heritage.

The poems are also occasionally arranged with an eye (and ear) to duets, trios, and quartets—brief conversations from poem to poem. For example, a section from 'Attar's famous *Convocation of the Birds* precedes Francis of Assisi's likewise celebrated *Canticle of the Creatures*—which in turn is followed by a contemporary Irish poet's musing on Francis's love of animals. There is also a small collection of poems about Mary in the Noon section (Noon because that is the hour tradition ascribes to the Annunciation).

The Psalms, which remain the great lyric treasure of Western monotheism, display an astonishing range of temper which this collection tries to mimic—everything from exultant praise and lighthearted joy to heartbroken lament, nasty calls for revenge and hopeless cries for mercy. This wild emotional compass is another of the cyclical oppositions that distinguish the Western relation to God, a cycle as constant as the cycle of night and day. This high emotional melodrama is a hallmark of the Western spiritual voice. For in its search for the sacred, the soul of the West is nothing if not moody.

The West, of course, includes much in its religious and mystical history besides monotheism. The animist beliefs of European pre-Christian times and of the Caribbean, Latin American, and North American Indian peoples have produced rich and beautiful poetry and chant that are alive today, sometimes playing cunningly at the edges, even penetrating, orthodox monotheism.

Still, it is worth framing poetry from the three great religions of "The Book" (if not the same book), the traditions known as the three "Abrahamic traditions," or as Gore Vidal has called them in exasperation, "the three sky-god religions of the West." They have been and remain the most resounding voices of Western culture.

Throughout history these three religions have spent much of their energy defining themselves against each other, emphasizing oppositions and differences, and when they could, imposing injunctions against each other. But even these attempts, often undertaken in violence, underscore their inevitable kinship.

Their mutual preoccupation with the Oneness of God and their insistence on putting all other gods (and of course goddesses) out of commission represent the single greatest communal effort of the Western imagination. It must be acknowledged: this monumental creative surge is also an act of repression, as the old gods are sacrificed to the One.

In recent times much attention has been given to the fateful spiritual choice the West made when it elected to find its God in heaven rather than in the rocks and trees of the inspirited earth. Every evil—from the genocide of whole populations to the despoiling of the earth—has been attributed to this portentous monotheistic will for Oneness.

"Before the coming of Christianity all the peoples of the Old World had lived in a numinous landscape spangled with sacred markers and sacred places," Frederick Turner writes in *Spirit of Place: The Making of an American Landscape.* "The land itself was believed to be alive and under the protection of numina, guardian spirits. In such a world," Turner points out, "one did not blithely cut down a grove of trees, plow up virgin meadowland, dam a stream or divert it."

And he goes on, "The gradual conquest of Europe by the Judeo-Christian worldview changed all this. The one and only God banished the thousands of local numina just as he had earlier banished Zeus and Saturn."

This sobering critique of monotheism is necessary to us as we search for the spiritual foundation that will guide our modern world crowded by its population and, even more, by its greed. Yet it has been our history, our Way—even our fate—to pursue the One God. In the Western mind, even today, the notion of divinity is so profoundly constellated as monotheistic that it is not simply the way of expressing belief, but the only real way of professing disbelief: No one asks, "Do you believe in the gods?" We ask each other if we believe in God.

Inevitable as the critique of the Western monotheistic tradition has been in recent years, it would be a mistake to be too eager to make an intellectual escape from this ancient tradition, as if one could think oneself away from one's own formation. Such intellectual distancing may be the latest Western version of salvation—to be saved from the ruins and ruining of one's own tradition by "deciding" what and how much of that tradition "works" and what does not.

But it is a salvation at odds with the longing for an abiding relation with existence outside one's own limitations. "Come to prayer," the muezzin cries from the minaret as he marks each day's portion of worship, "Come to security." This is not the security of thoughtlessness, but the harder shelter of tradition, of acquiescence to a spiritual discipline linking the individual not only to the world, but to history, to the dead who went before and to the yet unborn who will perform these same daily rituals when we too are the dead.

The urge toward monotheism, sustained over long centuries, is too protean to be seen as a plotted corporate takeover of the soul, monotheistic power brokers cynically divesting the world of its little people, its sprites and spirits, its gamboling gods and goddesses. Genuine passion drew the Western mind away from polytheism.

To acknowledge the resulting political and ecological evils attendant on monotheism is one of the requirements of our times. But to remain blind to the passion and beauty of its igniting impulse also betrays the impatience of a highly evolved individualistic intelligence faced with the mysterious and disquieting appetite for mystical surrender.

That mystical passion for Oneness encouraged a courageous, even outrageous, leap into the Unknown, a willingness to approach the abyss that mystics of East and West have always known to be the essence of the Divine. The One, they know, is Nothing. In a way hard for us to comprehend, encrusted as we are with centuries of institutional religion, early monotheism carried a frightening shock of irreverence. As the Cistercian writer David Steindl-Rast has said, the early Christians were not thrown to the lions because they were perceived as "believers." The charge against them was the refusal to worship the gods. They died branded as atheists.

Unless we can hear the urgency and longing that drew the Western mind toward the One True God against all the delights of a more rich and populated spirit realm, we miss knowing ourselves. We miss understanding the poignant craving for relation with The One and Only that occasioned the lonely search that lies at the heart of Western consciousness.

And we miss a glimpse of the Idea that unites the three warring populations of Western monotheism even today. Our own times force us to see, through wars and dislocation, just how profoundly enmeshed these three traditions are. They—We—fight to the death over an acre of desert ground, over a destroyed village.

As I write this, Christians and Muslims are killing each other's children in the name of their religions in Bosnia and Croatia. And the struggles between Jews and Muslims have defined the bloody history of the Middle East for generations. Even at peace, these three religious groups must share the same sacred ground for ceremonies on their holiest days as if they inhabited a single household. Like the relation of the rising of the sun to its setting, there is no getting away from each other.

In a time-honored practice, well worth invoking here, the editor of an anthology apologizes for the collection's limitations and omissions. Almost any anthology—especially one that ranges over centuries and cultures as this one does—calls for such a disclaimer. Certainly this slim volume cannot stake authority over its vast subject: sacred poetry from the West's three great monotheistic traditions, Judaism, Christianity, and Islam—to list them in their historical order of appearance. It does not pretend to be an "overview," and it definitely is not a compendium or survey.

But perhaps anthologies come by their limitations and idiosyncrasies honestly. No anthology, grounded in the fundamental definition of the word, can be in an aerial position to its subject, looking down and taking in the whole shape of the landscape. The original root of the word *anthology* reveals the subjective nature of such collections. Taken from the Greek, it means a collection of flowers [*antho* = flower + *logos*, adjective derived from *legein* = to pick, collect].

A charming etymology, but also an instructive one: Whoever gathers the flowers is in the field too, not above it. Vision is limited. The collection is made from what is within reach—or stretch. And once the gathering has begun, a sense of form and color—the bouquet itself—exercises an influence on what is chosen. An internal shape starts to emerge; it exerts its own demands, encouraging the development of *this* arrangement, not some other one.

There is also the fact of personal taste, always at the core of choice. The collecting is subjective, even casual, as truly independent reading always is, that luxurious browsing in stores and public libraries and secondhand stalls and other people's bookshelves with no authority but one's own hunger and hunches to lead the way. The editor is forced—I am certainly—to give up a convincing logic and simply admit: what was included was what was most loved from what came within reach by effort or by chance.

This collection does not attempt to analyze the connection among the three faiths, though it does assume a relation. The aim here is simple: to draw together, in the ancient sense of the word, a bouquet collected more or less at random, over time and geography, from the poetry of these three adjacent, overlapping, fields.

For an English-speaking reader, the three fields do not yield an equal harvest. It is still especially difficult to find substantial work translated from Muslim writers. On the other hand, a mystic poet as prolific as the Sufi sage Rumi has many translators and is represented here in several English translations and "versions."

What best represents Jewish poetry—ancient Hebrew? Modern Hebrew? Yiddish? Medieval Andalusian poetry? Contemporary American Jewish poets? Jewish poets writing in German? Before the Holocaust? After? And is the Holocaust, though so thoroughly a part of Jewish experience and history, also part of "the sacred"—or is it "political" with no place here?

As for Christian poetry—does that mean the Metaphysical Poets of the English Renaissance? A mystic like John of the

Cross? T.S. Eliot? Gabriela Mistral? Does Hopkins belong with Blake? With Auden? Does Wallace Stevens belong at all?

Yes, they all belong—or so this collection suggests. And what about the hallmark Western spiritual preoccupation of our own times, namely the persistent confession of disbelief? Does that belong to a consideration of "the sacred" too? Is Emily Dickinson writing a sacred poem when she begins one of her lyrics:

> *My period had come for Prayer—*
> *No other Art—would do—*
> *My Tactics missed a rudiment—*
> *Creator—Was it you?*

The modern spiritual consciousness recognizes this painful ambivalence. The loss of faith, the nostalgia for or fury against religion, are all part of the sacred. Not-knowing is at the heart of monotheism's encounter with the holy. And in the fundamental nervousness of monotheism—its inability to sustain faith in the Invisible One—all expressions of despair are very much part of what the experience of the sacred is.

So are expressions of simple distance or disjunction from a beloved tradition, one felt and acknowledged in the bones. Irish Catholic poets like Paul Murray express this attachment to a birthright. So does the great Israeli poet Yehuda Amichai comparing his life with his father's:

> *In the sands of prayer my father saw angels' traces.*
> *He saved me a space, but I wandered in other spaces.*
> *That's why his face was bright and why mine is scorched.*

Even the horrors of history belong to the sacred. The Holocaust, as written—even sung—by a poet as powerful as Nelly

Sachs belongs expressly to the tradition of the prophets of the hidden, singular God:

> *If the prophets broke in*
> *through the doors of night*
> *and sought an ear like a homeland—*
>
> *Ear of mankind*
> *overgrown with nettles,*
> *would you hear?*
> *If the voice of the prophets*
> *blew*
> *on flutes made of murdered children's bones*
> *and exhaled airs burnt with*
> *martyrs' cries—*
> *if they built a bridge of old men's drying*
> *groans—*
>
> *Ear of mankind*
> *occupied with small sounds,*
> *would you hear?*

But the other, even heavier, question resounding down the ages of monotheism is, *Does God hear?* Job, in his fury at the suffering God has rained down on him, spits out ragefully, "What difference does it make to you, man-watcher?" God as an aloof voyeur is the worst nightmare of monotheism. If the One God is a vicious sadist, if we are all the victims of this abusive Father, is there any hope for us? The Psalmist, the first poet of monotheism, tries to accept the situation (Psalm 8):

> *When I consider thy heavens, the word of thy fingers,*
> *The moon and the stars which thou hast ordained,*
> *What is man, that thou art mindful of him?*

Between the frightening absence of God and his apparent appetite for indiscriminate cruelty, lies the charge of poetry and its mysterious power to secure both truth and comfort. Even Job, hardly eager to sing an ode to his Creator, understands in the midst of his misery that this will to utterance belongs to the fundamental human impulse toward the Divine. He lists the appalling powers of the Lord God in all their overwhelming might, the very powers that have destroyed him (Book of Job 12:12–17):

> *Behold he destroyeth, and it cannot be built again;*
> *He shutteth up a man, and there can be no opening.*
>
> *Behold, he withholdeth the waters, and they dry up;*
> *Also he sendeth them out, and they overturn the earth.*
>
> *With him are strength and victory,*
> *The deceived and the deceiver are both his.*
>
> *He leadeth counsellors away stripped*
> *And of judges he maketh fools.*

But after this indictment Job does not turn away. Astonishingly, he says, with a mildness that seems an acknowledgement of his very nature as a human being, *"Notwithstanding I would speak to the Almighty."*

This impulse to speak to the Almighty, to cry out, to praise, to "reason with God," as Job puts it, still sparks the Western imagination, and still provides the solace grounded in reality that belongs to poetry and its readers.

The mystery of life, cloaked so guilelessly in day and night, makes the search for God the enduring human drama. We know so little, we feel so much. We have only the shape of our lives, experienced in the cycle of light and dark, to guide us toward meaning. But this is material enough for poets.

Rumi, perhaps the greatest (and certainly the most prolific) of the mystical poets, doesn't simply understand this essential dilemma of our existence. He embraces it as a daily practice, and implicitly beckons us to do so as well:

> *They say it's night,*
> > *but I don't know about day and night—*
> *I only know the face of that one*
> > *who fills the heavens with light.*
>
> *O night, you are dark because*
> > *you do not know Him,*
> *O day, go and learn from Him*
> > *what it means to shine.*

—SAINT PAUL, MINNESOTA
DECEMBER 1994

BURNING BRIGHT

MORNING

*I*NTROIT

This morning,
on entering the cold chapel,

    I looked first
to the sun, as the pagan does,
not by strict custom
nor by constraint, but because
    I too, as creature,
sense man's primitive emotion:
his need to praise.
And so, like priest or pagan,

    according
as the sun moves, I perform
this ancient ritual.
And though not always able

    to approach,
often, effaced in light, I stand
before this
chalice of the morning,

    I break this
ordinary bread as something holy.

—PAUL MURRAY

AND LOOK FOR GOD

I always lay before my rushing heart,
Never saw the morning,
Never sought God.
But now I wander about my child's
Gold-written limbs
And look for God.

I am weary from slumber;
Know of night's countenance only.
I'm afraid of the dawn;
It has a face
Like people with questions.

I always lay before my rushing heart;
But now I grope about my child's
God-lighted limbs.

—ELSE LASKER-SCHULER

#11

Like the rose I am laughing with all my body, not only with my mouth, because I am without myself, alone with the king of the world.

You who came with torch and at dawn ravished my heart, dispatch my soul after my heart, do not seize my heart alone.

Do not in rage and envy make my soul a stranger to my heart; do not leave the former here, and do not summon the latter alone.

Send a royal message, issue a general invitation; how long, O sultan, shall the one be with you and the other alone?

If you do not come tonight as yesterday and close my lips, I will make a hundred uproars, my soul, I will not lament alone.

—RUMI

GOD LOOKS ON NATURE WITH A GLORIOUS EYE

And blesses all creation with the sun
Its drapery of green and brown earth ocean lie
In morning as Creation just begun
That saffron east fortells the rising sun
And who can look upon that majesty
Of light brightness and splendour nor feel won
With love of him whose bright all seeing eye
Feeds the days light with Immortallity

—JOHN CLARE

I am happy to live correctly and simply:
Like the sun—like the pendulum—like the calendar.
To be a secular recluse, graceful
And wise—like the least of God's creatures.

Laws: the Spirit is my companion and guide!
To enter unannounced, like a ray, like a glance.
To live as I write: correctly and succinctly—
As God has enjoined, as my friends tell me not to.

—MARINA TSVETAEVA
   22 NOVEMBER 1919

$\mathcal{T}$HE BREATH OF NATURE

When great Nature sighs, we hear the winds
Which, noiseless in themselves,
Awaken voices from other beings,
Blowing on them.
From every opening
Loud voices sound. Have you not heard
This rush of tones?

There stands the overhanging wood
On the steep mountain:
Old trees with holes and cracks
Like snouts, maws, and ears,
Like beam-sockets, like goblets,
Grooves in the wood, hollows full of water:
You hear mooing and roaring, whistling,
Shouts of command, grumblings,
Deep drones, sad flutes.
One call awakens another in dialogue.
Gentle winds sing timidly,
Strong ones blast on without restraint.
Then the wind dies down. The openings
Empty out their last sound.
Have you not observed how all then trembles and subsides?

Yu replied: I understand:
The music of earth sings through a thousand holes.
The music of man is made on flutes and instruments.
What makes the music of heaven?

Master Ki said:
Something is blowing on a thousand different holes.
Some power stands behind all this and makes the sounds die down.
What is this power?

—CHAUNG TZU
TRANSLATED BY THOMAS MERTON

RIDDLE

Lord,
  whose face is this
    reflected in spirit's mirror?
    Such beauty painted
      on the inner screen—
      who is he?
Each atom
 in all space
 is filled . . .
    Who transcends the galaxies,
      shows himself in every molecule—
      who is he?
Sun
 in the costume
  of various specks of dust
   sparks forth various rays
    of light at every moment—
    who is he?
Outwardly
 you appear in the meat
  of our existence
   but he who is hidden
   in soul's marrow—
    who is he?

In soul's fete
  every now and again he sings
    a new song, melodies of peace
    touching the veils
      of the people of the heart—
      who is he?
He who manifests himself
  upon himself
    makes love to himself
    in the name
    of lovers—
    who is he?
How many times, Mo'in
  will you drag yourself and me
  between us?
    He, the goal of I and thou,
    is there—*right there!*
    Who is he?

—GHARIB NAWAZ

I FIND YOU, LORD, IN ALL THINGS AND IN ALL

I find you, Lord, in all Things and in all
my fellow creatures, pulsing with your life;
as a tiny seed you sleep in what is small
and in the vast you vastly yield yourself.

The wondrous game that power plays with Things
is to move in such submission through the world:
groping in roots and growing thick in trunks
and in treetops like a rising from the dead.

—RAINER MARIA RILKE

FLOWER IN THE CRANNIED WALL

Flower in the crannied wall,
I pluck you out of the crannies,
I hold you here, root and all, in my hand,
Little flower—but *if* I could understand
What you are, root and all, and all in all,
I should know what God and man is.

—ALFRED TENNYSON

REFLECTIONS AT LAKE LOUISE

I
At midnight the teacher lectures on his throne
Gongs, bells, wooden fish, tingling brass
Transcendent Doctrines, non-meditation, old dog barks
Past present future burn in Candleflame
incense fills intellects—
Mornings I wake, forgetting my dreams,
dreary hearted, lift my body out of bed
shave, wash, sit, bow down to the ground for hours.

II
Which country is real, mine or the teacher's?
Going back & forth I cross the Canada border, unguarded,
   guilty, smuggling 10,000 thoughts.

III
Sometimes my guru seems a Hell King, sometimes a King in
        Eternity,
   sometimes a newspaper story, sometimes familiar eyed
    father, lonely mother, hard working—
Poor man! to give me birth who may never grow up
   and earn my own living.

May 7, 1980

IV
Now the sky's clearer, clouds lifted, a patch of blue
shows above Mt. Victoria. I should go walking to the Plain of
                                          the Six Glaciers
but I have to eat Oryoki style, prostrate hours in the basement,
                                          study for
If I had a heart attack on the path around the lake would I be
                                          ready to face my mother?
                                          Noon

V
Scandal in the Buddhafields
        The lake's covered with soft ice inches thick.
Naked, he insulted me under the glacier!
        He raped my mind on the wet granite cliffs!
He misquoted me in the white mists all over the *Nation*.
Hurrah! the Clouds drift apart!
        Big chunks of blue sky fall down!
Mount Victoria stands with a mouth full of snow.

VI

I wander this path along little Lake Louise, the teacher's too busy
                                                          to see me,
my dharma friends think I'm crazy, or worse, a lonely neurotic,
                                                          maybe
Alone in the mountains, same as in snowy streets of New York.

VII

Trapped in the Guru's Chateau surrounded by 300 disciples
I could go home to Cherry Valley, Manhattan, Nevada City
to be a farmer forever, die in Lower East Side slums, sit with no
        lightbulbs in the forest,
Return to my daily mail Secretary, *Hard Times*, Junk mail and
        love letters, get wrinkled old in Manhattan
Fly out and sing poetry, bring home windmills, grow tomatoes and
                                                          Marijuana
chop wood, do Zazen, obey my friends, muse in Gary's Maidu
        Territory, study acorn mush,
Here I'm destined to study the Higher Tantras and be a slave to
        Enlightenment.
Where can I go, how choose? Either way my life stands before me,
mountains rising over the white lake 6 a.m., mist drifting
between water and sky.

                                                    May 7-9, 1980

—ALLEN GINSBERG

$\mathcal{P}$ S A L M

A psalm on the day
a building contractor cheated me. A psalm of praise.
Plaster falls from the ceiling, the wall is sick, paint
cracking like lips.

The vines I've sat under, the fig tree—
it's all just words. The rustling of the trees
creates an illusion of God and justice.

I dip my dry glance like bread
into the death that softens it,
always on the table in front of me.
Years ago, my life
turned my life into a revolving door.
I think about those who, in joy and success,
have gotten far ahead of me,
carried between two men for all to see
like that bunch of shiny pampered grapes
from the Promised Land,
and those who are carried off, also
between two men: wounded or dead. A psalm.

When I was a child I sang in the synagogue choir,
I sang till my voice broke. I sang
first voice and second voice. And I'll go on singing
till my heart breaks, first heart and second heart.
A psalm.

—YEHUDA AMICHAI

Praise to the Holy Creator, who has placed his throne upon the waters, and who has made all terrestrial creatures. To the Heavens he has given dominion and to the Earth dependence; to the Heavens he has given movement, and to the Earth uniform repose.

He raised the firmament above the earth as a tent, without pillars to uphold it. In six days he created the seven planets and with two letters he created the nine cupolas of the Heavens.

In the beginning he gilded the stars, so that at night the heavens might play tric-trac.

With diverse properties he endowed the net of the body, and he has put dust on the tail of the bird of the soul.

He made the Ocean liquid as a sign of bondage, and the mountain tops are capped with ice for fear of him.

He dried up the bed of the sea and from its stones brought forth rubies, and from its blood, musk.

To the mountains he has given peaks for a dagger, and valleys for a belt; so that they lift up their heads in pride. . . .

Sun and Moon—one the day, the other the night, bow to the dust in adoration; and from their worship comes their movement. It is God who has spread out the day in whiteness, it is he who has folded up the night and blackened it. . . .

When he breathes on clay man is created; and from a little vapor he forms the world. . . .

In winter he scatters the silver snow; in autumn, the gold of yellow leaves.

He lays a cover on the thorn and tinges it with the color of blood.

To the jasmine he gives four petals and on the head of the tulip he puts a red bonnet.

He places a golden crown on the brow of the narcissus; and drops pearls of dew into her shrine.

At the idea of God the mind is baffled, reason fails; because of God the heavens turn, the earth reels.

From the back of the fish to the moon every atom is a witness to his Being.

The depths of earth and the heights of heaven render him each their particular homage.

God produced the wind, the earth, the fire, and blood, and by these he announces his secret.

His throne is on the waters and the world is in the air. But leave the waters and the air, for all is God: the throne and the world are only a talisman. God is all, and things have only a nominal value; the world visible and the world invisible are only Himself.

—'ATTAR

$\mathcal{T}$HE CANTICLE OF BROTHER SUN

Most High, all-powerful, good Lord,
Yours are the praises, the glory, the honor, and all blessing.
To You alone, Most High, do they belong,
and no man is worthy to mention Your name.
Praised be You, my Lord, with all your creatures,
especially Sir Brother Sun,
Who is the day and through whom You give us light.
And he is beautiful and radiant with great splendor;
and bears a likeness of You, Most high One.
Praised be You, my Lord, through Sister Moon and the stars, in heaven
You formed them clear and precious and beautiful.
Praised be you, my Lord, through Brother Wind,
and through the air, cloudy and serene, and every kind of weather
through which You give sustenance to Your creatures.
Praised be You, my Lord, through Sister Water,
which is very useful and humble and precious and chaste.
Praised be You, my Lord, through Brother Fire,
through whom You light the night
and he is beautiful and playful and robust and strong.
Praised be You, my Lord, through our Sister Mother Earth,
who sustains and governs us,
and who produces varied fruits with colored flowers and herbs.

Praised be You, my Lord, through those who give pardon for
Your love
and bear infirmity and tribulation.
Blessed are those who endure in peace
for by You, Most High, they shall be crowned.

Praised be You, my Lord, through our Sister Bodily Death,
from whom no living man can escape.
Woe to those who die in mortal sin.
Blessed are those whom death will find in Your most holy will,
for the second death shall do them no harm.
Praise and bless my Lord and give Him thanks
and serve Him with great humility.

—FRANCIS OF ASSISI

$\mathcal{P}$ROBLEM

I understand Francis—all the stuff about the birds,
Throwing his clothes at his father; the singing, praising Heart.

Once I travelled from Rome into Umbria
To his town, his green mountains,
His fast streams,

Saw the coarse cloth he wore against cold,
The chapel shrining Chiara's hair.

Teresa Sanchez was never a problem:
In convent or covered wagon
In constant seesaw up and down towards God.

Or John
Soaring through his bars like a linnet in song.

But I am blind still to the Jew
My life traipses after;

And the spacelessness of God
Hesitates the hand I reach
Behind cross and tabernacle

Into his paltry loneliness.

—PADRAIG J. DALY

$\mathcal{S}$IMONE WEIL: IN ASSISI

To stand on the parcel of land where the saint
knelt down and married Lady Poverty, to walk
through the grasses of the Umbrian hills
where he scolded wolves and preached

to doves and jackdaws, where he chanted
canticles to the creatures who share our earth,
praising Brother Sun who rules the day,
Sister Moon who brightens the night.

Brother Fire sleeps in the arms of Sister Water.
Brother Wind kisses Sister Earth so tenderly.
To carry a picnic and eat whatever he ate—

bread and wine, the fare of tourists and saints.

She disliked the Miracles in the Gospels.
She never believed in the mystery of contact,
here below, between a human being and God.
She despised popular tales of apparitions.

But that afternoon in Assisi she wandered
through the abominable Santa Maria degli Angeli
and happened upon a little marvel of Romanesque
purity where St. Francis liked to pray.

She was there a short time when something absolute
and omnivorous, something she neither believed
nor disbelieved, something she understood—
but what was it?—forced her to her knees.

—EDWARD HIRSCH

QUATRAIN

He Who splashed a thousand worlds with color
How can He buy the paint of "I and thou"?
Colors, colors—nothing but whim and fantasy;
HE is colorless, and one must adopt His hue.

—'AYN AL-QOZAT HAMADANI

LUZZATO

PADUA 1717

The sentences we studied are rungs upon the ladder Jacob saw;
the law itself is nothing but the road;
I have become impatient of what the rabbis said,
and try to listen to what the angels say.
I have left Padua and am in Jerusalem at last, my friend;
for, as our God was never of wood or bone,
our land is not of stones or earth.

—CHARLES REZNIKOFF

GOOD FRIDAY

This is the day, the cock has crowed
the passing of dreams, the death-cold dawn,
the setting of the star of Bethlehem
behind a brow of stone.

This is the day the cock crowed in,
crowed out the night; the lovers straying
beyond the body's grasp, now must return
each entering his dimension like a tomb.

This is the hour of cock-crow and the men
whose night was out of bounds, clock in again,
(as innocent in sleep as plant or stone)
wake to do wrong, grow old, and suffer pain.

The cock crows out the night, and we remain
outside eternity, the lover's dream
the soldier's sleep, the locked gates of the tomb,
ghosts of our days, longing for night again.

—KATHLEEN RAINE

$\mathcal{T}$HE THIRD DAY

When they came to the tomb
What did they see?
Only what they could not say.

Too empty, too cold
To say what they saw,
Too full to say empty

And cold, but full
They said what they said,
Saw what they saw,

And knew they could not
Say what they saw.
They did not know

That whatever words they found
To say would fill the world
With those very words,

The best they could find
In that place, that time,
When all words fail or fall.

After the stone is rolled away,
After the sky refuses to reply,
Comes the heaviness of being here.

—PHILLIS LEVIN

FROM
*I*NTIMATE CONVERSATIONS
WITH GOD

O God,
I have bound myself to you to the exclusion of all else.
If you would have me, I will worship you.
If you would have me not, I will worship myself.
Make me not despondent: Take my hand!

O God,
If I am raw, cook me!
If I am cooked, burn me!

O God,
Your reckoning is with those who have,
and I am a dervish.
If your accounting is with paupers,
then I come before anyone else.

O God,
What value have I to be worthy of you?
If you will, chastise me.
If you will, forgive me.
You hold the key: How should I open the door?

—KWAJA ABDULLAH ANSARI

7. Lauds
Among the leaves the small birds sing;
The crow of the cock commands awaking:
In solitude, for company.

Bright shines the sun on creatures mortal;
Men of their neighbors become sensible:
In solitude, for company.

The crow of the cock commands awaking;
Already the mass-bell goes dong-ding:
In solitude, for company.

Men of their neighbors become sensible;
God bless the Realm, God bless the People:
In solitude, for company.

God bless the Realm, God bless the People;
God bless this green world temporal:
In solitude, for company.

The dripping mill-wheel is again turning;
Among the leaves the small birds sing:
In solitude, for company.

—W.H. AUDEN

O N A N G E L S

All was taken away from you: white dresses,
wings, even existence.
Yet I believe you,
messengers.

There, where the world is turned inside out,
a heavy fabric embroidered with stars and beasts,
you stroll, inspecting the trustworthy seams.

Short is your stay here:
now and then at a matinal hour, if the sky is clear,
in a melody repeated by a bird,
or in the smell of apples at the close of day
when the light makes the orchards magic.

They say somebody has invented you
but to me this does not sound convincing
for humans invented themselves as well.

The voice—no doubt it is a valid proof,
as it can belong only to radiant creatures,
weightless and winged (after all, why not?),
girdled with the lightning.

I have heard that voice many a time when asleep
and, what is strange, I understood more or less
an order or an appeal in an unearthly tongue:

day draws near
another one
do what you can.

—CZESLAW MILOSZ

3 9

Come, come, for the rosebower has blossomed; come, come, for the beloved has arrived.

Bring at once altogether soul and world; deliver over to the sun, for the sun has drawn a fine blade.

Laugh at that ugly one showing off airs; weep for that friend who is severed from the Friend.

The whole city seethed when the rumour ran abroad that the madman had once again escaped from his chains.

What day is it, what day is it, such a day of uprising?— Perchance the scroll of men's deeds has already fluttered from the skies.

Beat the drums, and speak no more; what place is there for heart and mind? For the soul too has fled.

—RUMI

*G*OD'S GRANDEUR

The world is charged with the grandeur of God.
    It will flame out, like shining from shook foil;
It gathers to a greatness, like the ooze of oil
Crushed. Why do men then now not reck his rod?
Generations have trod, have trod, have trod;
    And all is seared with trade; bleared, smeared with toil;
    And wears man's smudge and shares man's smell: the soil
Is bare now, nor can foot feel, being shod.

And for all this, nature is never spent;
    There lives the dearest freshness deep down things;
And though the last lights off the black West went
    Oh, morning, at the brown brink eastward, springs—
Because the Holy Ghost over the bent
    World broods with warm breast and with ah! bright wings.

—GERARD MANLEY HOPKINS

HIDDEN NAME

The true Name is not the one that gilds portals, illustrates proceedings; nor the one the populace chews with vexation;

The true Name is not to be read in the Palace itself, nor in gardens or grottos, but remains hidden in the waters under an aqueduct I drink from.

Only when there is great drought, when frostbound winter crackles, when springs, at their lowest ebb, spiral in shells of ice,

When the void gapes underground in the heart's cavern—where blood itself has ceased to flow—under the vault, now accessible, the Name can be received.

But let the hard waters melt, let life overflow, let the devastating torrent surge rather than Knowledge!

—VICTOR SEGALEN

$\mathcal{L}$OST

This god who has gaped ever since we created him
and shrined him in the sky
I wish he had never spoken
but only opened his heart and arms
to embrace those
who created him
and made him a legend.
I wish his shadow had stayed
uncolored by the world
his silhouette had remained
untouched by motion,
his words had lasted
without being eaten
and re-eaten.

Instead he mutinied against his creator
wanted him to be the created
and man was lost between two creations—
      his creation of the god
      and the god's creation of him
still, creator and created
became a single destiny,
marching as one
toward a new creation
that is still beyond us.

—ORKHAN MUYASSAR

When the wind sacks the village
Twisting the cries
The bird
Is engulfed in the sun

All is ruin
And ruin
A spiritual contour

—MICHEL DEGUY

3.
You I give no name to
The mysterious things within you
are an untrodden bower
over whose earthen orbit
planets move harboring
constellations of beauty.

4.
You I give no name to
The mysterious things within you
are fragrance, light and melody
housed in flesh and blood
a sacred beacon that reveals
God's shadow.

6.
The mysterious things within you
are a legend in my heart
With them I've built my castle
In them I've dug my grave
Drunk or sober I've loved them
They've comforted me
on my lonely way
hard as rock
If the mysterious things within you
were not strings for me to play on
I'd still have been their song.

—AHMAD AL-MUSHARI AL-'UDWANI

*T*HE PULLEY

When God at first made man,
Having a glass of blessings standing by,
Let us (said he) pour on him all we can:
Let the world's riches, which dispersed lie,
　　Contract into a span.

So strength first made a way;
Then beauty flow'd, then wisdom, honour, pleasure:
When almost all was out, God made a stay,
Perceiving that, alone of all his treasure,
　　Rest in the bottom lay.

For if I should (said he)
Bestow this jewel also on my creature,
He would adore my gifts instead of me,
And rest in Nature, not the God of Nature:
　　So both should losers be.

Yet let him keep the rest,
But keep them with repining restlessness;
Let him be rich and weary, that at least,
If goodness lead him not, yet weariness
　　May toss him to my breast.

—GEORGE HERBERT

ON A BED OF GUERNSEY LILIES

Ye beauties! O how great the sum
    Of sweetness that ye bring;
On what a charity ye come
    To bless the latter spring!

How kind the visit that ye pay,
Like strangers on a rainy day,
    When heartiness despair'd of guests:
No neighbour's praise your pride alarms,
No rival flow'r surveys your charms,
    Or heightens, or contests!

Lo, thro' her works gay nature grieves
    How brief she is and frail,
As ever o'er the falling leaves
    Autumnal winds prevail.
Yet still the philosophic mind
Consolatory food can find,
    And hope her anchorage maintain:
We never are deserted quite;
'Tis by succession of delight
    That love supports his reign.

—CHRISTOPHER SMART

I NVOCATION

New falconer
    teach heart's hawk
        the hunt of Thought
teach
    tongue's nightingale
        to invoke the Name;
the tongue
    (that fish
        in the mouth's fountain)
will relish the taste
    of divine
        remembrance.
Heart's theriac:
    to repeat and repeat
        "There is no God but HE"
—but the heart
    must remain awake—otherwise
        it's nothing but hullabaloo.
Foster the spirit
    with remembrance—only then
        the heart finds peace in the Name,
His Name
    written in the
        Book of Unity,
the eternal
    Alchemy
        of Happiness.

—SANA'I

---

[15]

Your image, tormenting and elusive,
I could not touch in the mist.
"God!" I said by mistake,
never thinking to say that myself.

God's name like a gigantic bird
flew out from my breast.
Before me thick mist swarms,
behind me stands an empty cage.

—OSIP MANDELSTAM

$\mathcal{S}$UNDAY MORNING

I.
Complacencies of the peignoir, and late
Coffee and oranges in a sunny chair,
And the green freedom of a cockatoo
Upon a rug mingle to dissipate
The holy hush of ancient sacrifice.
She dreams a little, and she feels the dark
Encroachment of that old catastrophe,
As a clam darkens among water-lights.
The pungent oranges and bright, green wings
Seem things in some procession of the dead,
Winding across wide water, without sound.
The day is like wide water, without sound,
Stilled for the passing of her dreaming feet
Over the seas, to silent Palestine,
Dominion of the blood and sepulchre.

II.

Why should she give her bounty to the dead?
What is divinity if it can come
Only in silent shadows and in dreams?
Shall she not find in comforts of the sun,
In pungent fruit and bright, green wings, or else
In any blame or beauty of the earth,
Things to be cherished like the thought of heaven?
Divinity must live within herself:
Passions of rain, or moods in falling snow;
Grievings in loneliness, or unsubdued
Elations when the forest blooms; gusty
Emotions on wet roads on autumn nights;
All pleasures and all pains, remembering
The bough of summer and the winter branch.
These are the measures destined for her soul.

III.

Jove in the clouds had his unhuman birth
No mother suckled him, no sweet land gave
Large-mannered motions to his mythy mind.
He moved among us, as a muttering king,
Magnificent, would move among his hinds,
Until our blood, commingling, virginal,
With heaven, brought such requital to desire
The very hinds discerned it, in a star.
Shall our blood fail? Or shall it come to be
The blood of paradise? And shall the earth
Seem all of paradise that we shall know?
The sky will be much friendlier then than now,
A part of labor and a part of pain
And next in glory to enduring love,
Not this dividing and indifferent blue.

IV.
She says, "I am content when wakened birds,
Before they fly, test the reality
Of misty fields, by their sweet questionings;
But when the birds are gone, and their warm fields
Return no more, where, then, is paradise?"
There is not any haunt of prophecy,
Nor any old chimera of the grave,
Neither the golden underground, nor isle
Melodious, where spirits gat them home,
Nor visionary south, nor cloudy palm
Remote on heaven's hill, that has endured
As April's green endures; or will endure
Like her remembrance of awakened birds,
Or her desire for June and evening, tipped
By the consummation of the swallow's wings.

V.

She says, "But in contentment I still feel
The need of some imperishable bliss."
Death is the mother of beauty; hence from her,
Alone, shall come fulfilment to our dreams
And our desires. Although she strews the leaves
Of sure obliteration on our paths,
The path sick sorrow took, the many paths
Where triumph rang its brassy phrase, or love
Whispered a little out of tenderness,
She makes the willow shiver in the sun
For maidens who were wont to sit and gaze
Upon the grass, relinquished to their feet.
She causes boys to pile new plums and pears
On disregarded plate. The maidens taste
And stray impassioned in the littering leaves.

VI.

Is there no change of death in paradise?
Does ripe fruit never fall? Or do the boughs
Hang always heavy in that perfect sky,
Unchanging, yet so like our perishing earth,
With rivers like our own that seek for seas
They never find, the same receding shores
That never touch with inarticulate pang?
Why set the pear upon those river-banks
Or spice the shores with odors of the plum?
Alas, that they should wear our colors there,
The silken weavings of our afternoons,
And pick the strings of our insipid lutes!
Death is the mother of beauty, mystical,
Within whose burning bosom we devise
Our earthly mothers waiting, sleeplessly.

VII.
Supple and turbulent, a ring of men
Shall chant in orgy on a summer morn
Their boisterous devotion to the sun,
Not as a god, but as a god might be,
Naked among them, like a savage source.
Their chant shall be a chant of paradise,
Out of their blood, returning to the sky;
And in their chant shall enter, voice by voice,
The windy lake wherein their lord delights,
The trees, like serafin, and echoing hills,
That choir among themselves long afterward.
They shall know well the heavenly fellowship
Of men that perish and of summer morn.
And whence they came and whither they shall go
The dew upon their feet shall manifest.

VIII.

She hears, upon that water without sound,
A voice that cries, "The tomb in Palestine
Is not the porch of spirits lingering.
It is the grave of Jesus, where he lay."
We live in an old chaos of the sun,
Or old dependency of day and night,
Or island solitude, unsponsored, free,
Of that wide water, inescapable.
Deer walk upon our mountains, and the quail
Whistle about us their spontaneous cries;
Sweet berries ripen in the wilderness;
And, in the isolation of the sky,
At evening, casual flocks of pigeons make
Ambiguous undulations as they sink,
Downward to darkness, on extended wings.

—WALLACE STEVENS

Noon

ANGELUS

I see the blue, the green, the golden and the red,
I have forgotten all the angel said.

The flower, the leaf, the meadow and the tree,
but of the words I have no memory.

I hear the swift, the martin, and the wren,
but what was told me, past all thought is gone.

The dove, the rainbow, echo, and the wind,
but of the meaning, all is out of mind.

Only I know he spoke the word that sings its way
in my blood streaming, over rocks to sea,

A word engraved in the bone, that burns within
to apotheosis the substance of a dream,

That living I shall never hear again,
because I pass, I pass, while dreams remain.

—KATHLEEN RAINE

$\mathcal{T}$HE HOUSE

The table, son, is laid
with the quiet whiteness of cream,
and on four walls ceramics
gleam blue, glint light.
Here is the salt, here the oil,
in the center, bread that almost speaks.
Gold more lovely than gold of bread
is not in broom plant or fruit,
and its scent of wheat and oven
gives unfailing joy.
We break bread, little son, together
with our hard fingers, our soft palms,
while you stare in astonishment
that black earth brings forth a white flower.

Lower your hand that reaches for food
as your mother also lowers hers.
Wheat, my son, is of air,
of sunlight and hoe;
but their bread, called "the face of God,"*
is not set on every table.
And if other children do not have it,
better, my son, that you not touch it,
 better that you do not take it with ashamed hands.

*In Chile, the people call bread "the face of God." (G.M.)

My son, Hunger with his grimaced face
in eddies circles the unthrashed wheat.
They search and never find each other,
Bread and hunchbacked Hunger.
So that he find it if he should enter now,
we'll leave the bread until tomorrow.
Let the blazing fire mark the door
that the Quechaun Indian never closed,
and we will watch Hunger eat
to sleep with body and soul.

—GABRIELA MISTRAL

Land O'Lakes, Wisconsin:
Vajrayana Seminary

Candle light blue banners incense
aching knee, hungry mouth—
any minute the gone—potatoes and sour cream!

Sunlight on the red zafu,
clank of forks & plates—
I'll never be enlightened.

*

Did you ever see yourself
a breathing skull
looking out the eyes?

*

Under wooden roof beams
a hundred people
sit
sniffling, coughing, clearing throat
sneezing, sighing
breathing through nose
shifting on pillows in clothes
swallowing saliva,
listening.

November 11, 1976

—ALLEN GINSBERG

I FOUND IT

I found it on a radiant day
after a long drifting.
It was green and blossoming
as the sun over palm trees
scattered golden bouquets;
April was generous that season
with loving and sun.

I found it
after a long wandering.
It was a tender evergreen bough
where birds took shelter,
a bough bending gently under storms
which later was straight again,
rich with sap,
never snapping in the wind's hand.
It stayed supple
as if there were no bad weather,
echoing the brightness of stars,
the gentle breeze,
the dew and the clouds.

I found it
on a vivid summer day
after a long straying,
a tedious search.
It was a quiet lake
where thirsty human wolves
and swirling winds could only briefly
disturb the waters.
Then they would clear again like crystal
to be the moon's mirror,
swimming place of light and blue,
bathing pool for the guardian stars.

I found it!
And now when the storms wail
and the face of the sun is masked in clouds,
when my shining fate revolves to dark,
my light will never be extinguished!
Everything that shadowed my life
wrapping it with night after night
has disappeared, lain down
in memory's grave,
since the day
my soul found
my soul.

—FADWA TUQAN

$\mathcal{F}$OR SONG

I am sitting thirty feet above the water
with my hand at my throat,
listening to the owls go through the maples
and the seaplanes go up and down like cracked buzzsaws.

I am finding my own place in the scheme of things
between the nation of Reuben half drunk on twisted coneflowers
and the nation of Dan all crazy for weird veronica.

I am paying attention to providence,
the silver hordes this time,
the mud up to my knees,
the glass on my fingers.

I am studying paradise and the hereafter,
a life beyond compare,
a great log thrown up for my own pleasure,
an unbelievably large and cold and beneficent sun.

I am lifting a blade of grass to my wet lips
for music;
I am trying a dozen fruits and flowers
to get one sound;

I am twisting my head around, I am slowly clapping
for harmony;
I am raising my eyes, I am listening to the worms
for song.

—GERALD STERN

6 2 3

It was too late for Man—
But early, yet, for God—
Creation—impotent to help—
But Prayer—remained—Our Side—

How excellent the Heaven—
When Earth—cannot be had—
How hospitable—then—the face
Of our Old Neighbor—God—

—EMILY DICKINSON

$\mathcal{T}$ WELVE LINES ABOUT
THE BURNING BUSH

What's going to be the end for both of us—God?
Are you really going to let me die like this
and really not tell me the big secret?

Must I really become dust, gray dust, and ash, black ash,
while the secret, which is closer than my shirt, than my skin,
still remains secret, though it's deeper in me than my own heart?

And was it really in vain that I hoped by day and waited by night?
And will you, until the very last moment, remain godlike-cruel
        and hard?
Your face deaf like dumb stone, like cement, blind-stubborn?

Not for nothing is one of your thousand names—thorn, you
        thorn in my spirit and flesh and bone,
piercing me—I can't tear you out; burning me—I can't stamp
        you out,
moment I can't forget, eternity I can't comprehend.

—MELECH RAVITCH

$\mathcal{A}$UTUMN

The thistle down's flying Though the winds are all still
On the green grass now lying Now mounting the hill
The spring from the fountain Now boils like a pot
Through stones past the counting It bubbles red hot

The ground parched and cracked is Like over baked bread
The greensward all wrecked is Bent dried up and dead
The fallow fields glitter Like water indeed
And gossamers twitter Flung from weed unto weed

Hill tops like hot iron Glitter hot i' the sun
And the Rivers we're eyeing Burn to gold as they run
Burning hot is the ground Liquid gold is the air
Who ever looks round Sees Eternity there

—JOHN CLARE

*G*OOD FRIDAY, 1613.
RIDING WESTWARD

Let man's soul be a sphere, and then, in this,
The intelligence that moves, devotion is,
And as the other Spheres, by being grown
Subject to foreign motions, lose their own,
And being by others hurried every day,
Scarce in a year their natural form obey:
Pleasure or business, so, our souls admit
For their first mover, and are whirl'd by it.
Hence is 't, that I am carried towards the west
This day, when my soul's form bends toward the east.
There I should see a sun, by rising set,
And by that setting endless day beget;
But that Christ on this cross, did rise and fall,
Sin had eternally benighted all.
Yet dare I almost be glad, I do not see
That spectacle of too much weight for me.
Who sees God's face, that is self life, must die;
What a death were it then to see God die?
It made his own lieutenant, Nature, shrink,
It made his footstool crack, and the sun wink.
Could I behold those hands which span the poles,
And turn all spheres at once, pierc'd with those holes?
Could I behold that endless height which is
Zenith to us, and our Antipodes,
Humbled below us? or that blood which is
The seat of all our souls, if not of his,
Made dirt of dust, or that flesh which was worn

But God, for his apparel, ragg'd, and torn?
If on these things I durst not look, durst I
Upon his miserable mother cast mine eye,
Who was God's partner here, and furnish'd thus
Half of that sacrifice, which ransom'd us?
Though these things, as I ride be from mine eye,
They are present yet unto my memory,
For that looks towards them; and thou look'st towards me,
O Savior, as thou hang'st upon the tree;
I turn my back to thee, but to receive
Corrections, till thy mercies bid thee leave.
O think me worth thine anger, punish me,
Burn off my rusts, and my deformity,
Restore thine image, so much, by thy grace,
That thou may'st know me, and I'll turn my face.

—JOHN DONNE

$\mathcal{P}$ SALM

No one moulds us again out of earth and clay,
no one conjures our dust.
No one.

Praised be your name, no one.
For your sake
we shall flower
Towards
you.

A nothing
we were, are, shall
remain, flowering;
the nothing-, the
no one's rose.

With our pistil soul-bright
with our stamen heaven-ravaged
our corolla red
with the crimson word which we sang
over, o over
the thorn

—PAUL CELAN

LESS AND LESS HUMAN,
O SAVAGE SPIRIT

If there must be a god in the house, must be,
Saying things in the rooms and on the stair,

Let him move as the sunlight moves on the floor,
Or moonlight, silently, as Plato's ghost

Or Aristotle's skeleton. Let him hang out
His stars on the wall. He must swell quietly.

He must be incapable of speaking, closed,
As those are: as light, for all its motion, is;

As color, even the closest to us, is;
As shapes, though they portend us, are.

It is the human that is the alien,
The human that has no cousin in the moon.

It is the human that demands his speech
From beasts or from the incommunicable mass.

If there must be a god in the house, let him be one
That will not hear us when we speak: a coolness,

A vermilioned nothingness, any stick of the mass
Of which we are too distantly a part.

—WALLACE STEVENS

The blind woman was more intimate with it
than any one of us.

They took her to the beach
and left her there alone.
She turned her face toward
the sea's blue voice,
she smiled and sank
in contemplation.

Its outline ran across the sand,
inscribed in children's clamor.
Breath by breath, she took its amplitude,
and prayer by prayer its pulse.
It glistened tear-like on an eyelash, then

with its wet fingers on her face
the horizon read what was
beyond its line.

—BLAGA DIMITROVA

$\mathcal{A}$N ANDALUSIAN EXILE

O bird crying on the acacia tree, alike are our sorrows
Should I grieve for your troubles or lament my own?
What tale have you to tell me?—only that the self-same hand
That laid my heart waste has pinioned your wing.
Exile has cast us both, fellow strangers,
In a grove not our own, where our kind never meet
Parting has struck us—you with a knife, me with a barbed arrow.
Roused by longing, neither of us can move,
our broken wings too weak to answer our will.
Child of the valley, nature has set us apart,
and yet affliction has brought us together.
You have not forsaken your drink for unquenched longing,
Sad memory, or countless similar sorrows,
Dragging your feet on the boughs, and your tail behind you,
You go in search of one who might heal you.
There are many to heal the body if we but seek them,
But where, O where the skillful healer of the soul?

—AHMAD SHAUQI

She was there on the mountain,
still as the fig tree and the failed wheat.
Only the lizards and a few goats moved.
Everything stunned by heat and silence.
I would get to the top of the terraced starkness
with my ankles cut by thistles and all of me
drained by the effort in the fierce light.
I would put the pomegranate and the anise
and a few daisies on the great rock
where the fountain was long ago.
Too tired to praise. And found each time
tenderness and abundance in the bareness.
Went back down knowing I would sleep clean.
That She would be awake all year with sun
and dirt and rain. Pride Her life.
All nature Her wealth. Sound of owls Her pillow.

—LINDA GREGG

*I*MMACULATE CONCEPTION

FOR EILEEN COWIN

It was not love. No flowers or ripened figs
were in his hands, no words
in his mouth. There was no body
to obstruct us from each other.
The sun was white-hot, a brand
that sank through me and left no mark.
Yet I knew. And Joseph,
poor Joseph with his thick palms,
wearing antlers.
What could he do but wash
the scorched smell from the linen?
What could he do but fit the blades
of wood together into a cradle?

The rain fell and the leaves closed
over us like a shield.
A small light formed and the taper
that held it aloft
was dipped many times into my blood.
Now the being rests in the bowl of my hips.
There is no turning. Already
the nails are forged.
The tree thickens.

—LOUISE ERDRICH

MARY

this kiss
as soft as cotton

over my breasts
all shiny bright

something is in this night
oh Lord have mercy on me

i feel a garden
in my mouth

between my legs
i see a tree

—LUCILLE CLIFTON

THE MOTHER OF GOD

The threefold terror of love; a fallen flare
Through the hollow of an ear;
Wings beating about the room;
The terror of all terrors that I bore
The Heavens in my womb.

Had I not found content among the shows
Every common woman knows,
Chimney corner, garden walk,
Or rocky cistern where we tread the clothes
And gather all the talk?

What is this flesh I purchased with my pains,
This fallen star my milk sustains,
This love that makes my heart's blood stop
Or strikes a sudden chill into my bones
And bids my hair stand up?

—WILLIAM BUTLER YEATS

LILIES

I have been thinking
about living
like the lilies
that blow in the fields.

They rise and fall
in the wedge of the wind,
and have no shelter
from the tongues of the cattle,

and have no closets or cupboards,
and have no legs.
Still I would like to be
as wonderful

as that old idea.
But if I were a lily
I think I would wait all day
for the green face

of the hummingbird
to touch me.
What I mean is,
could I forget myself

even in those feathery fields?
When Van Gogh
preached to the poor
of course he wanted to save someone—

most of all himself.
He wasn't a lily,
and wandering through the bright fields
only gave him more ideas

it would take his life to solve.
I think I will always be lonely
in this world, where the cattle
gaze like a black and white river—

where the ravishing lilies
melt, without protest, on their tongues—
where the hummingbird, whenever there is a fuss,
just rises and floats away.

—MARY OLIVER

THE DIVINE IMAGE

To Mercy Pity Peace and Love,
All pray in their distress:
And to these virtues of delight
Return their thankfulness.

For Mercy Pity Peace and Love,
Is God our father dear:
And Mercy Pity Peace and Love,
Is Man his child and care.

For Mercy has a human heart
Pity, a human face:
And Love, the human form divine,
And Peace, the human dress.

Then every man of every clime,
That prays in his distress,
Prays to the human form divine
Love Mercy Pity Peace.

And all must love the human form,
In heathen, turk or jew.
Where Mercy, Love & Pity dwell
There God is dwelling too.

—WILLIAM BLAKE

$\mathcal{H}$OLY WELL

In the annals saints
Sit in holy wells, talk freely
To grim hermits, heal
Who ails, the foot-holy
Pilgrims who walk in wishes.

The dumb speak, the cripple
Walks, the blind
Find the dazzling world of the mind
In new pigments. Here
The ways of God seem wayward but very dear.

Speak the word, Saint
In your welling mineral
That world in a bright and single jet
Go up, and inside it, lit up,
God my space and my material.

—PADRAIC FALLON

ᴀɴᴅ ᴛʜᴀᴛ ɪѕ ʏᴏᴜʀ ɢʟᴏʀʏ

(Phrase from the liturgy of the Days of Awe)

I've yoked together my large silence and my small outcry
like an ox and an ass. I've been through low and through high.
I've been in Jerusalem, in Rome. And perhaps in Mecca anon.
But now God is hiding, and man cries Where have you gone.
And that is your glory.

Underneath the world, God lies stretched on his back,
always repairing, always things get out of whack.
I wanted to see him all, but I see no more
than the soles of his shoes and I'm sadder than I was before.
And that is his glory.

Even the trees went out once to choose a king.
A thousand times I've given my life one more fling.
At the end of the street somebody stands and picks:
this one and this one and this one and this one and this.
And that is your glory.

Perhaps like an ancient statue that has no arms
our life, without deeds and heroes, has greater charms.
Ungird my T-shirt, love; this was my final bout.
I fought all the knights, until the electricity gave out.
And that is my glory.

Rest your mind, it ran with me all the way,
it's exhausted now and needs to knock off for the day.
I see you standing by the wide-open fridge door, revealed
from head to toe in a light from another world.
And that is my glory
and that is his glory
and that is your glory.

—YEHUDA AMICHAI

$\mathcal{L}$OVE POEM

In your quest or request God is remote.
Yet He alone can be your anchor and your space,
the pulse and the parts,
the vine and the separation.

If God were a man, I would touch His robe
and burn into Him.
If He were a man, I would kiss His feet
and kneel or lie before Him.
I would cry, bleed, die . . .
But He is not a man,
not a body.

You yourself are God because He made you,
classified you, gifted you and sailed within you.
You yourself are God because He sees you,
knows you, speaks to you,
enlightens you, bears you,
throws you, treads on you,
scatters and sunders and bolts with you.
You yourself are God because you exist.
The world is a moth in God's hands,
and the moth is greater and more beautiful
than you because it is
smaller and larger than you.

Between you and God are time and light.
Between you and God are sun and stars.
Between you and God are heaven and all
created things.

But God is not you, and you know best that God is not
because you are naked without God.
His fingers stretch from your head to your heart.
His hands are in your blood.
Your face and all the seas are but a bit of sand.
Yet you say you are God!
Do you dare to say that you will kiss God's robe,
God's chest, God's feet?
Do you dare to say that you are God, and God is you?
Do you dare?
Do you dare?

—HUDA NA'MANI

$\mathcal{L}$ O V E

Love bade me welcome; yet my soul drew back,
      Guilty of dust and sin.
But quick-eyed Love, observing me grow slack
      From my first entrance in,
Drew nearer to me, sweetly questioning,
      If I lacked anything.

"A guest," I answered, "worthy to be here."
      Love said, "You shall be he."
"I, the unkind, ungrateful? Ah, my dear,
      I cannot look on thee."
Love took my hand, and smiling did reply,
      "Who made the eyes but I?"

"Truth, Lord, but I have marred them; let my shame
      Go where it doth deserve."
"And know you not," says Love, "who bore the blame?"
      "My dear, then I will serve."
"You must sit down," says Love, "and taste my meat."
      So I did sit and eat.

—GEORGE HERBERT

QUICKNESS

False life! a foil and no more, when
                      Wilt thou be gone?
Thou foul deception of all men
That would not have the true come on.

Thou art a moonlike toil; a blind
                      Self-posing state;
A dark contest of waves and wind;
A mere tempestuous debate.

Life is a fix'd, discerning light,
                      A knowing joy;
No chance, or fit: but ever bright,
And calm and full, yet doth not cloy.

'Tis such a blissful thing, that still
                      Doth vivify,
And shine and smile, and hath the skill
To please without Eternity.

Thou art a toilsome mole, or less,
                      A moving mist,
But life is, what none can express,
A quickness, which my God hath kiss'd.

—HENRY VAUGHAN

My period had come for Prayer—
No other Art—would do—
My Tactics missed a rudiment—
Creator—Was it you?

God grows above—so those who pray
Horizons—must ascend—
And so I stepped upon the North
To see this Curious Friend—

His House was not—no sign had He—
By Chimney—nor by Door
Could I infer his Residence—
Vast Prairies of Air

Unbroken by a Settler—
Were all that I could see—
Infinitude—Had'st Thou no Face
That I might look on Thee?

The Silence condescended—
Creation stopped—for Me—
But awed beyond my errand—
I worshipped—did not "pray"—

—EMILY DICKINSON

I HAVE FAITH

I have faith in all those things that are not yet said.
I want to set free my most holy feelings.
What no one has dared to want
will be for me impossible to refuse.

If that is presumption, then, my God, forgive me.
However, I want to tell you this one thing:
I want my best strength to be like a shoot,
with no anger and no timidity, as a shoot is;
this is the way the children love you.

With these ebbing tides, with these mouths
opening their deltas into the open sea,
with these returns, that keep growing,
I want to acknowledge you, I want to announce you,
as no one ever has before.

And if that is arrogance, then I will stay arrogant
for the sake of my prayer,
that is so sincere and solitary
standing before your cloudy forehead.

—RAINER MARIA RILKE

INSATIABLENESS

I.
No walls confine! Can nothing hold my mind?
     Can I no rest nor satisfaction find?
          Must I behold eternity
               And see
          What things above the Heav'ns be?
               Will nothing serve the turn?
               Nor earth, nor seas, nor skies?
                    Till I what lies
               In time's beginning find;
          Must I till then for ever burn?

Not all the crowns; not all the heaps of gold
On earth; not all the tales that can be told,
     Will satisfaction yield to me:
                    Nor tree,
          Nor shade, nor sun, nor Eden, be
               A joy: nor gems in gold,
               (Be't pearl or precious stone,)
                    Nor spring, nor flowers,
               Answer my craving powers,
     Nor anything that eyes behold.

Till I what was before all time descry,
The world's beginning seems but vanity.
     My soul doth there long thoughts extend;
               No end
     Doth find, or being comprehend:
                    Yet somewhat sees that is
                    The obscure shady face
                         Of endless space,
                    All room within; where I
     Expect to meet eternal bliss.

II.

This busy, vast, inquiring soul
                    Brooks no control,
                No limits will endure,
        Nor any rest: it will all see,
Not time alone, but ev'n eternity.
            What is it? Endless sure.
                    'Tis mean ambition to desire
                A single world:
            To many I aspire,
                Though one upon another hurl'd:
        Nor will they all, if they be all confin'd,
                    Delight my mind.

This busy, vast, inquiring soul
                    Brooks no control:
                'Tis very curious too.
        Each one of all those worlds must be
Enriched with infinite variety
                    And worth; or 'twill not do.

        'Tis nor delight nor perfect pleasure
                    To have a purse
            That hath a bottom in its treasure,
Since I must thence endless expense disburse.
Sure there's a God (for else there's no delight)
                    One infinite.

—THOMAS TRAHERNE

Lord hear my prayer when trouble glooms
Let sorrow find a way
And when the day of trouble comes
Turn not thy face away
My bones like hearth stones burn away
My life like vapoury smoke decays

My heart is smitten like the grass
That withered lies and dead
And I so lost to what I was
Forget to eat my bread
My voice is groaning all the day
My bones prick through this skin of clay

The wildernesses pelican
The deserts lonely owl
I am there like a desert man
In ways as lone and foul
As sparrows on the cottage top
I wait till I with faintness drop

I bear my enemies reproach
All silently I mourn
They on my private peace encroach
Against me they are sworn
Ashes as bread my trouble shares
And mix my food with weeping cares

Yet not for them is sorrows toil
I fear no mortals frown
But thou hast held me up awhile
And thou hast cast me down
My days like shadows waste from view
I mourn like withered grass in dew

But thou Lord shalt endure forever
All generations through
Thou shalt to Zion be the giver
Of joy and mercey too
Her very stones are in their trust
Thy servants reverence her dust

Heathens shall hear and fear thy name
All kings of earth thy glory know
When thou shalt build up Zions fame
And live in glory there below
He'll not despise their prayers though mute
But still regard the destitute.

—JOHN CLARE

A whole afternoon field inside me from one stem of reed.
The messenger comes running toward me, irritated:
Why be so hard to find?

Last night I asked the moon about the Moon, my one question
for the visible world, Where is God?
The moon says, *I am dust stirred up
when he passed by.* The sun, *My face is pale yellow
from just now seeing him.* Water, *I slide on my head and face
like a snake, from a spell he said.* Fire, *His lightning,
I want to be that restless.* Wind, why so light?
I would burn if I had a choice. Earth, quiet
and thoughtful? *Inside me I have a garden
and an underground spring.*

This world hurts my head with its answers,
wine filling my hand, not my glass.
If I could wake completely, I would say without speaking
why I'm ashamed of using words.

—RUMI

DIPTYCH: JESUS AND THE STONE

1.
The gold in *Jesus and the Stone* fell
to the painter's brush from a faithful afterlife,
homeland of dyes and tinted doors,

but where is Jesus? In the background
of this medieval altar-piece, the stone stands wide
for the gap where Christ once was but isn't

anymore, nor is he on the icy mountains
or the scared blunt sea. Jesus isn't there
and yet a crowd has gathered, foreground, all

odd proportions with knobby faces and wooden
trunks, bearded, two-dimensioned figures pointing
meaning: where? where? Cobalt blue

stains the frightened market woman's dress,
and her starched white veil guards suspicions
that death is only just and finally death.

2.

                         But there, almost hidden
in the pointing crowd, right foreground,
is the returning son of man, familiar
halo like a guarantee of joyous fire

and maybe a faint smile, and maybe not
because the artist has been vague about the face
he loves; he was on his knees

and when he came to him, he fell back,
not knowing how to fill it in, that whole,
God's gold face. Two dots. A line. Astonished tears.

—CHARLES BAXTER

*I*MAGINARY CAREER

At first a childhood, limitless and free
of any goals. Ah sweet unconsciousness.
Then sudden terror, schoolrooms, slavery,
the plunge into temptation and deep loss.

Defiance. The child bent becomes the bender,
inflicts on others what he once went through.
Loved, feared, rescuer, wrestler, victor,
he takes his vengeance, blow by blow.

And now in vast, cold, empty space, alone.
Yet hidden deep within the grown-up heart,
a longing for the first world, the ancient one . . .

Then, from His place of ambush, God leapt out.

—RAINER MARIA RILKE

$\mathcal{T}$HREAD SUNS

above the grey-black wilderness.
A tree-
high thought
tunes in to light's pitch: there are
still songs to be sung on the other side
of mankind.

—PAUL CELAN

NIGHT

FINAL SOLILOQUY OF THE INTERIOR PARAMOUR

Light the first light of evening, as in a room
In which we rest and, for small reason, think
The world imagined is the ultimate good.

This is, therefore, the intensest rendezvous.
It is in that thought that we collect ourselves,
Out of all the indifferences, into one thing:

Within a single thing, a single shawl
Wrapped tightly round us, since we are poor, a warmth,
A light, a power, the miraculous influence.

Here, now, we forget each other and ourselves.
We feel the obscurity of an order, a whole,
A knowledge, that which arranged the rendezvous.

Within its vital boundary, in the mind.
We say God and the imagination are one . . .
How high that highest candle lights the dark

Out of this same light, out of the central mind,
We make a dwelling in the evening air,
In which being there together is enough.

—WALLACE STEVENS

$\mathcal{T}$HE COURSE OF A LIFE

Till eight days like any happy fly,
on the eighth, a Jew.
To be circumcised,
to learn pain without words.

In childhood, a Catholic
for the dances of ritual and its games,
the splendor of fear, the glory of sin
and shining things up above,

or a Jew for the commandments of Shalt and Shalt Not.
We begged you, Lord, to divide right from wrong
and instead you divided the waters above the firmament
from those beneath it. We begged
for the knowledge of good and evil, and you gave us
all kinds of rules like the rules of soccer.

A young man believes in nothing and loves everything,
worships idols and stars, worships girls,
worships hope, despair.

A Protestant at the age when toughening sets in,
the cheek and the mouth, wheeling and dealing, upper
and lower jaw, commerce and industry.

But after midnight, everyone's the muezzin
of his own life, calling out from the top of himself
as if from the top of a minaret,
crying parched from the agony of the desert
about the failure of flesh and of blood,
howling lusts that have never been fulfilled.

Afterward, a motley crowd, you and I, religions
of oblivion and religions of memory,
hot baths, sunsets and a quiet drunkenness
till the body is soul and the soul, body.

And toward the end, again a Jew,
served up on a white pillow to the *sandak*
after the pain, from him to a good woman
and from one good woman to another,
the taste of sweet wine on his lips, and the taste
of pain between his legs.

And the last eight days without
consciousness, without knowledge, without belief
like any animal, like any stone,
like any happy fly.

—YEHUDA AMICHAI

I bless the everyday labor,
I bless the nightly rest.
God's mercy and God's judgment,
A good law—and a stony law.

And my dusty purple, where so many holes,
And my dusty staff, where all the rays . . .
—And, Lord, I bless as well the peace
In a stranger's house—and the bread in a stranger's oven.

—MARINA TSVETAEVA
   21 MAY 1918

THE FORTUNE TELLER

She points to a star
that shows you your other shadow.
You see in a single poem
the fact of God, the fact of earth
and everything between the two.

You see a dove
that sleeps like any vagabond
in crevices, or rides the lightning
until it rests in a blue cloud
moored on its own seas.

You seek a new map.

—FU'AD RIFQA

ONLY FOR YOU

The sky wears in a belt of clouds
The bended moon.

Under the sickle image
I want to rest within your hand.

I always have to do the will of the storm;
As a sea without shore.

But since you seek my seashells
My heart glows.

It lies at the bottom of me
Under a spell.

Perhaps my heart is the world,
Beats—

And searches only for you—
How should I call you?

—ELSE LASKER-SCHULER

CELESTIAL MUSIC

I have a friend who still believes in heaven.
Not a stupid person, yet with all she knows, she literally talks to god,
she thinks someone listens in heaven.
On earth, she's unusually competent.
Brave, too, able to face unpleasantness.

We found a caterpillar dying in the dirt, greedy ants crawling
over it.
I'm always moved by weakness, by disaster, always eager to
oppose vitality.
But timid, also, quick to shut my eyes.
Whereas my friend was able to watch, to let events play out
according to nature. For my sake, she intervened, brushing a
few ants off the torn thing, and set it down across the road.

My friend says I shut my eyes to god, that nothing else explains
my aversion to reality. She says I'm like the child who buries her
head in the pillow so as not to see, the child who tells herself
that light causes sadness—
My friend is like the mother. Patient, urging me
to wake up an adult like herself, a courageous person—

In my dreams, my friend reproaches me. We're walking
on the same road, except it's winter now;
she's telling me that when you love the world you hear celestial
music: look up, she says. When I look up, nothing.
Only clouds, snow, a white business in the trees
like brides leaping to a great height—
Then I'm afraid for her; I see her
caught in a net deliberately cast over the earth—

In reality, we sit by the side of the road, watching the sun set;
from time to time, the silence pierced by a birdcall.
It's this moment we're both trying to explain, the fact
that we're at ease with death, with solitude.
My friend draws a circle in the dirt; inside, the caterpillar doesn't
move.
She's always trying to make something whole, something
beautiful, an image
capable of life apart from her.
We're very quiet. It's peaceful sitting here, not speaking, the
composition fixed, the road turning suddenly dark, the air
going cool, here and there the rocks shining and glittering—
it's this stillness that we both love.
The love of form is a love of endings.

—LOUISE GLÜCK

THE PIOUS ONE

I must see the lighthouse keeper,
go to his craggy rock
feel the wave break in his mouth,
see the abyss in his eyes.
I want to find him, if he lives,
that old salt man of sea.

They say he looks only eastward,
walled-up alive at sea.
When I shatter his wave, I wish
he would turn his eyes from the abyss to me.

He knows all there is to know of night
which has become my bed and path;
he knows the octopus, sponge, and undertow,
and the senses slain by a scream.

His chastened breast
is spat upon by tides,
is shrilled by gulls,
is white as the maimed.
So still, so mute and unmindful
as though unborn.

But I go to the lighthouse tower
to climb the knife-edged path
and be with the man who will tell me
what is earthly and what divine.
In one arm I bring him a jug of milk,
in the other, a sip of wine.

On he goes listening to seas
in love with nothing but themselves.
Perhaps now he listens to nothing,
fixed in forgetfulness and salt.

—GABRIELA MISTRAL

*I*F THE PROPHETS BROKE IN

If the prophets broke in
through the doors of night,
the zodiac of demon gods
wound like a ghastly wreath of flowers
round the head—
rocking the secrets of the falling and rising
skies on their shoulders—

for those who long since fled in terror—

If the prophets broke in
through the doors of night,
the course of the stars scored in their palms
glowing golden—

for those long sunk in sleep—

If the prophets broke in
through the doors of night
tearing wounds with their words
into fields of habit,
a distant crop hauled home
for the laborer

who no longer waits at evening—

If the prophets broke in
through the doors of night
and sought an ear like a homeland—

Ear of mankind
overgrown with nettles,
would you hear?
If the voice of the prophets
blew
on flutes made of murdered children's bones
and exhaled airs burnt with
martyrs' cries—
if they built a bridge of old men's dying
groans—

Ear of mankind
occupied with small sounds,
would you hear?

If the prophets
rushed in with the storm-pinions of eternity
if they broke open your acoustic duct with the words:
Which of you wants to make war against a mystery
who wants to invent the star-death?

If the prophets stood up
in the night of mankind
like lovers who seek the heart of the beloved,
night of mankind
would you have a heart to offer?

—NELLY SACHS

$\mathcal{T}$HE MONK

He tramped in the fading light
Of a late February day
Between hedges stiff with the wind.
Rough folds of his robe swung.
His boots trod stone and clay.
His blown habit crouched
In the wet daylight's decay.
A spade across his shoulder
Slanted into the sky.
Sunk in the cowl his quiet eye.

A sense of scrubbed flesh in the path;
A thought of washing in cold hours
When dreams are scrubbed off
In a chill room, huge flowers,
Night blooms, accidentally plucked,
Each dawn devours;
Of a haggard taste in the mouth
Savouring in death a tide of light,
Harvest in all decay,
Spring in February night.

—THOMAS KINSELLA

A FOOTNOTE ON MONASTICISM: DINGLE PENINSULA

In certain places, still, surprisingly, you come
Upon them, resting like old straw hats set down
Beside the sea, weather-beaten but enduring
For a dozen centuries; here the mound
That was the roof has slithered in
And the outlines you can barely trace:
Nor does it matter since every wilderness
Along this coast retains more signs
In ragged groupings of these cells and caves
Of where the hermits, fiercely dispossessed,
Found refuge among gulls and rocks
The incessant prayer of nearby waves.

Among darkening rocks he prayed,
Body chastened and absurd,
An earth-bound dragging space
His spirit blundered like a bird:
Hands, specialised by prayer,
Like uplifted chalices,
Nightly proffering the self
To soundless, perfect messengers.

There are times, certainly, looking through a window
At amiable clustered humanity, or scanning
The leaves of some old book, that one might wish
To join their number, start a new and fashionable
Sect beside the Celtic sea, long favourable
To dreams and dreamers; anchorites whose love
Was selfishly alone, a matter so great
That only to stone could they whisper it:
Breaking the obstinate structure of flesh
With routine of vigil and fast,
Till water-cress stirred on the palate
Like the movement of a ghost.

In ceaseless labour of the spirit,
Isolate, unblessed;
Until quietude of the senses
Announces presence of a guest;
Desolation final,
Rock within and rock without
Till from the stubborn rock of the heart
The purifying waters spurt.

—JOHN MONTAGUE

Entangled . . .

Entangled in so many stars,
From which I gradually free myself,
I feel my laws take shape
In the disorder of the skies.
The earth's solitude
And my own are mingled.
Ah! none is more alone than God
In his heart's great pit.

Someone somewhere
Must live and breathe
And without quite realizing it
Be my companion:
Let him know in his heart
In spite of its evasions that I exist;
Let him set me up on high,
And let me not yield to him,

I who shall be in him forever.

—JULES SUPERVIELLE

$\mathcal{T}$HE TYGER

Tyger Tyger, burning bright,
In the forests of the night;
What immortal hand or eye,
Could frame thy fearful symmetry?

In what distant deeps or skies
Burnt the fire of thine eyes!
On what wings dare he aspire?
What the hand, dare seize the fire?

And what shoulder, & what art,
Could twist the sinews of thy heart?
And when thy heart began to beat,
What dread hand? & what dread feet?

What the hammer? what the chain,
In what furnace was thy brain?
What the anvil? what dread grasp,
Dare its deadly terrors clasp?

When the stars threw down their spears
And water'd heaven with their tears:
Did he smile his work to see?
Did he who made the Lamb make thee?

Tyger, Tyger burning bright,
In the forests of the night:
What immortal hand or eye,
Dare frame thy fearful symmetry?

—WILLIAM BLAKE

LONELINESS

at night
yes night
when walls start breathing
and concrete fogs spread
seeping between fingers, into nostrils
when we find no one to talk to
when in vain we search out wrinkled faces, scarred hands
when in rooms hermetically sealed we scream
where echo does not echo
when we raise our hands and no shadow falls
when at the door we hear no knock
and none pass beneath the window
when we hear no marmots gnaw in the cupboard
or love groan in the next room
when we rush to the dresser drawer
but fail to find the family photo album
when we look for a gun, knife or rope
yet hit only plaster wall
which in total silence cracks
when we think of our names but do not think of them
when all this happens alone at night, God,
in a sealed room
what shall we do?

—AMJAD NASIR

$\mathcal{P}$RAYER

The laws of blind unrest, not art,
Have built this room in time and space,
The furniture of human sense
That bounds my sorrow, curbs delight.

But to the grail, these fragile walls
Are thinner than a floating dream,
And here the heart's full measure fills
With what is worldwide, yet within.

And gathering round me those I know
In the close circle of a prayer,
The sleepers, the forgetful, grow
In love, though not in presence, near.

My distant ones, this heart on fire
Is for a candle in your night,
While you lie safe within that care
Whose dark is sleep, whose waking, light.

—KATHLEEN RAINE

FROM
*J*UBILATE AGNO

For the word of God is a sword on my side—no matter what other
 weapon a stick or a straw.

For I have adventured myself in the name of the Lord, and he hath
 mark'd me for his own.

For I bless God for the Postmaster general & all conveyancers of
 letters under his care especially Allen & Shelvock.

For my grounds in New Canaan shall infinitely compensate for
 the flats & maynes of Staindrop Moor.

For the praise of God can give to a mute fish the notes of a
 nightingale.

For I have seen the White Rave & Thomas Hall of Willingham &
 am myself a greater curiosity than both.

For I look up to heaven which is my prospect to escape envy by
 surmounting it.

For if Pharaoh had known Joseph, he would have blessed God &
 me for the illumination of the people.

For I pray God to bless improvements in gardening till London
 be a city of palm-trees.

For I pray to give his grace to the poor of England, that Charity
 be not offended & that benevolence may increase.

For in my nature I quested for beauty, but God, God hath sent
 me to sea for pearls.

—CHRISTOPHER SMART

$\mathcal{T}$HE DARK NIGHT

One dark night,
Fired with love's urgent longings
Ah, the sheer grace!
I went out unseen,
My house being now all stilled;

In darkness, and secure,
But the secret ladder, disguised,
Ah, the sheer grace!
In darkness and concealment,
My house being now all stilled;

On that glad night,
In secret, for no one saw me,
Nor did I look at anything,
With no other light or guide

Than the one that burned in my heart;
This guided me
More surely than the light of noon
To where He waited for me
Him I knew so well
In a place where no one else appeared.

O guiding night!
O night more lovely than the dawn!
O night that has united
The Lover with His beloved,
Transforming the beloved in her Lover.

Upon my flowering breast
Which I kept wholly for Him alone,
There He lay sleeping,
And I caressing Him
There in a breeze from the fanning cedars.

When the breeze blew from the turret
Parting His hair,
He wounded my neck
With his gentle hand,
Suspending all my senses.
I abandoned and forgot myself,
Laying my face on my Beloved;
All things ceased; I went out from myself,
Leaving my cares
Forgotten among the lilies.

—JOHN OF THE CROSS

TRYING TO PRAY

This time, I have left my body behind me, crying
In its dark thorns.
Still,
There are good things in this world.
It is dusk.
It is the good darkness
Of women's hands that touch loaves.
The spirit of a tree begins to move.
I touch leaves.
I close my eyes, and think of water.

—JAMES WRIGHT

$\mathcal{T}$HE MOON AND THE YEW TREE

This is the light of the mind, cold and planetary.
The trees of the mind are black. The light is blue.
The grasses unload their griefs on my feet as if I were God,
Prickling my ankles and murmuring of their humility.
Fumy, spiritous mists inhabit this place
Separated from my house by a row of headstones.
I simply cannot see where there is to get to.

The moon is no door. It is a face in its own right,
White as a knuckle and terribly upset.
It drags the sea after it like a dark crime; it is quiet
With the O-gape of complete despair. I live here.
Twice on Sunday, the bells startle the sky—
Eight great tongues affirming the Resurrection.
At the end, they soberly bong out their names.

The yew tree points up. It has a Gothic shape.
The eyes lift after it and find the moon.
The moon is my mother. She is not sweet like Mary.
Her garments unloose small bats and owls.
How I would like to believe in tenderness—
The face of the effigy, gentled by candles,
Bending, on me in particular, its mild eyes.

I have fallen a long way. Clouds are flowering
Blue and mystical over the face of the stars.
Inside the church, the saints will be all blue,
Floating on their delicate feet over the cold pews,
Their hands and faces stiff with holiness.
The moon sees nothing of this. She is bald and wild.
And the message of the yew tree is blackness—
$\qquad\qquad\qquad$ blackness and silence.

—SYLVIA PLATH

$\mathcal{A}$ THIEF IN THE NIGHT

Suddenly
    (yet somehow expected)
he arrived
    the guest . . .
the heart trembling
    "Who's there?"
    and soul responding
        "The Moon . . ."

came into the house
    and we lunatics
ran into the street
    started up
        looking
           for the moon.

Then—inside the house—
    he cried out
"Here I am!"
    and we
beyond earshot
    running around
        calling him . . .
crying for him
    for the drunken nightingale
locked lamenting
    in our garden
while we
    mourning ringdoves
        murmured "Where
           where?"

As if at midnight
        the sleepers bolt upright
in their beds
        hearing a thief
break into the house
        in the darkness
they stumble about
        crying "Help!
                A thief! A thief!"
but the burglar himself
        mingles in the confusion
echoing their cries:
        ". . . a thief!"
                till one cry
                        melts with the others.

And He is with you
        with you
in your search
        when you seek Him
look for Him
        in your looking
closer to you
        than yourself
                to yourself;

Why run outside?
     Melt like snow
wash yourself
     with yourself:
urged by Love
     tongues sprout
from the soul
     like stamens
          from the lily . . .

But learn
     this custom
from the flower:
     Silence
          your tongue.

—RUMI

RIDING OUT AT EVENING

At dusk, everything blurs and softens.
From here out over the long valley,
the fields and hills pull up
the first slight sheets of evening,
as, over the next hour,
heavier, darker ones will follow.

Quieted roads, predictable deer
browsing in a neighbor's field, another's
herd of heifers, the kitchen lights
starting in many windows. On horseback
I take it in, neither visitor
nor intruder, but kin passing, closer
and closer to night, its cold streams
rising in the sugarbush and hollow.

Half-aloud, I say to the horse,
or myself, or whoever: let fire not come
to this house, nor that barn,
nor lightning strike the cattle.
Let dogs not gain the gravid doe, let the lights
of the rooms convey what they seem to.

And who is to say it is useless
or foolish to ride out in the falling light
alone, wishing, or praying,
for particular good to particular beings
on one small road in a huge world?
The horse bears me along, like grace,

making me better than what I am,
and what I think or say or see
is whole in these moments, is neither
small nor broken. For up, out of
the inscrutable earth, have come my body
and the separate body of the mare:
flawed and aching and wronged. Who then
is better made to say *be well, be glad,*

or who to long that we, as one,
might course over the entire valley,
over all valleys, as a bird in a great embrace
of flight, who presses against her breast,
in grief and tenderness,
the whole weeping body of the world?

—LINDA McCARRISTON

CARRION COMFORT

Not, I'll not, carrion comfort, Despair, not feast on thee;
Not untwist—slack they may be—these last strands of man
In me or, most weary, cry *I can no more.* I can;
Can something, hope, wish day come, not choose not to be.
But ah, but O thou terrible, why wouldst thou rude on me
Thy wring-world right foot rock? lay a lionlimb against me? scan
With darksome devouring eyes my bruised bones? and fan,
O in turns of tempest, me heaped there; me frantic to avoid thee
and flee?

Why? That my chaff might fly; my grain lie, sheer and clear.
Nay in all that toil, that coil, since (seems) I kissed the rod,
Hand rather, my heart lo! lapped strength, stole joy, would
laugh, cheer.
Cheer whom though? the hero whose heaven-handling flung me,
foot trod
Me? or me that fought him. O which one? is it each one?
          That night, that year
Of now done darkness I wretch lay wrestling with (my God!) my
God.

—GERARD MANLEY HOPKINS

Someone
will take the ball
from the hands that play
the game of terror.

Stars
have their own law of fire
and their fertility
is the light
and reapers and harvesters
are not native here.

Far off
stand their granaries
straw too
has a momentary power of illumination
painting loneliness.

Someone will come
and sew the green of the spring bud
on their prayer shawl
and set the child's silken curl
as a sign
on the brow of the century.

Here Amen
must be said
this crowning of words
which moves into hiding
and peace
you great eyelid
closing on all unrest
your heavenly wreath of lashes

You most gentle of all birds.

—NELLY SACHS

ZURICH, THE STORK INN

FOR NELLY SACHS

Of too much was our talk, of
too little. Of the You
and You-Again, of
how clarity troubles, of
Jewishness, of
your God.

Of
that.
On the day of an ascension, the
Minister stood over there, it sent
some gold across the water.

Of your God was our talk, I spoke
against him, I
let the heart that I had
hope:
for
his highest, death-rattled, his
quarrelling word—

Your eye looked on, looked away,
your mouth
spoke its way to the eye, and I heard:

We
don't know, you know,
we
don't know, do we?,
what
counts.

—PAUL CELAN

Song for the Moon

Are you a glass of milk, rich and cold?
Or a stream flowing with mother of pearl?

Or a white ripple of the twilight time
Sweetly crossing the face of night?

Or a jar, colored and dewy
A honey jar for all who are hungry?

Or are you a cheek of fragrant lilies
Dozing over grass and fallen leaves?

Or are you silver, lightlike and supple?
Ah, the glow of my old enchantment!

*

What are you? A vessel of light
A blending of stars out of the dark

Oh, kiss of lilies pouring out clear
The honey of a perfumed evening

You are a refuge and a haunt for beauty
A bouquet of lilies clasped by the sky

Your lips of light have come so close
To caressing the face of these fresh arbors

Oh pool of goodness and perfume
Sloping to the horizon, a basket of jasmine

*

The lovers' ferry bears them beyond
The lazy ocean and the sea of dream

On your nimble feathery wing
Strewing the path of passion with hope

Your spring spills slumber on any eye
Made sleepless by a lover's longing

You nourish those soft eyes with visions
Tilting your cup of toxic sleep
Oh, your finger, caressing wounds
Sowing songs and sprinkling kisses!

*

An island in the gloom, suspended
Dawnlike its propitious shade

Floating over an ambrosial stream
Flanked by magic starry shoes

Light has frozen on the shore
A cradle of silk, a crystal treasure

Oh, penitence of ugliness, Oh sail
of love, colorful and finely featured

The dark's heartache, the night's regret
Oh, atonement of the storm clouds!

*

Melt the fragments of rays and visions
at night, immerse our roofs in silver

Shake your tender wings in space
And the colors flow from the butterfly

Thanks to you the shadows dance
And the frail lilies' cups are cooled

You wove our dreams and suckled us
With your sweet flickering flashing light

You are dawn's window when night is spent
You feed the flowers that fill the meadows

*

Stay as you are, a secret world
Not such a thing as a soul discerns

Spinner of poems, the last muse
In a world whose mirrors are all dimmed

What song did not flow with honey
If you were to smile your praise upon it?

Joy was granted to song by you,
You, the weighted weaving pulse

Stay beyond life, in dreams, with love
Stay with poetry, and with God above

—NAZIK AL-MALA'IKA

I A M

1.

I am—yet what I am, none cares or knows;
     My friends forsake me like a memory lost:—
I am the self-consumer of my woes;—
     They rise and vanish in oblivion's host,
Like shadows in love's frenzied stifled throes:—
And yet I am, and live—like vapours tost

2.

Into the nothingness of scorn and noise,—
     Into the living sear of waking dreams,
Where there is neither sense of life or joys,
     But the vast shipwreck of my life's esteems;
Even the dearest, that I love the best
Are strange—nay, rather stranger than the rest.

3.

I long for scenes, where man hath never trod
     A place where woman never smiled or wept
There to abide with my Creator, God;
     And sleep as I in childhood, sweetly slept,
Untroubling, and untroubled where I lie,
The grass below—above the vaulted sky.

—JOHN CLARE

CHORUS OF THE STARS

We stars, we stars
We wandering, glistening, singing dust—
Earth, our sister, has gone blind
Among the constellations of heaven—
A scream she has become
Among the singers—
She, richest in longing
Who began her task—to form angels—in dust,
She whose secret contains bliss
Like streams bearing gold—
Poured out into the night she lies
Like wine in the streets—
Evil's yellow sulfur lights flicker over her body.

O earth, earth
Star of stars
Veined by the spoors of homesickness
Begun by God Himself—
Have you no one who remembers your youth?
No one who will surrender himself as the swimmer
To the oceans of death?
Has no one's longing ripened
So it will rise like the angelically flying seed
Of the dandelion blossom?

Earth, earth, have you gone blind
Before the sister eyes of the Pleiades
Or Libra's examining gaze?
Murder hands gave Israel a mirror
In which it recognized its death while dying—

Earth, O earth
Star of stars
One day a constellation will be called *mirror*.
Then, O blind one, you will see again!

—NELLY SACHS

ROCKING

The sea rocks her thousands of waves.
The sea is divine.
Hearing the loving sea
I rock my son.

The wind wandering by night
rocks the wheat.
Hearing the loving wind
I rock my son.

God, the Father, soundlessly rocks
His thousands of worlds.
Feeling His hand in the shadow
I rock my son.

—GABRIELA MISTRAL

O GOD

Only a brief sleep everywhere
In man, in the green, in the cup of the winds.
Everyone goes home to his dead heart.

—I wish the world were still a child—
And was able to tell me how it first drew breath.

One time there was great piety in heaven;
The stars passed the Bible around to read.
If only I could take God's hand sometime
Or see on his finger the spinning moon.

O God, O God, how far I am from you!

—ELSE LASKER-SCHULER

INTO THE FOGHORN

Mouth in the hidden mirror,
knee at the pillar of pride,
hand with the bar of a cage:

proffer yourselves the dark,
speak my name,
lead me to him.

—PAUL CELAN

Just as the Watchman

Just as the watchman in the wine fields
has a shed for himself and keeps awake,
I am the shed in your arms, Lord,
my night is drawn from your night.

Vineyard, meadow, weathered apple orchard,
field that never lets a spring go by,
fig tree rooted in ground hard
as marble, yet carrying a hundred figs:

odor pours out from your heavy boughs,
and you never ask if I am keeping watch or not;
confident, dissolved by the juices, your depths
keep climbing past me silently.

—RAINER MARIA RILKE

POEMS FROM A DIARY

1974

Who will last? And what? The wind will stay
and the blind man's blindness when he's gone away,
and a thread of foam—a sign of the sea—
and a bit of cloud snarled in a tree.

Who will last? And what? word as green
as Genesis, making grasses grow.
And what the prideful rose might mean,
Seven of those grasses know.

Of all that northflung starry stuff,
the star descended in the tear will last.
In its jar, a drop of wine stands fast.
Who lasts? God abides—isn't that enough?

—ABRAHAM SUTZKEVER

RIBH CONSIDERS CHRISTIAN LOVE INSUFFICIENT

Why should I seek for love or study it?
It is of God and passes human wit.
I study hatred with great diligence,
For that's a passion in my own control,
A sort of besom that can clear the soul
Of everything that is not mind or sense.

Why do I hate man, woman or event?
That is a light my jealous soul has sent.
From terror and deception freed it can
Discover impurities, can show at last
How soul may walk when all such things are past,
How soul could walk before such things began.

Then my delivered soul herself shall learn
A darker knowledge and in hatred turn
From every thought of God mankind has had.
Thought is a garment and the soul's a bride
That cannot in that trash and tinsel hide: Hatred of God
may bring the soul to God.

At stroke of midnight soul cannot endure
A bodily or mental furniture.
What can she take until her Master give!
Where can she know until He bid her know!
How can she live till in her blood He live!

—WILLIAM BUTLER YEATS

World, Do Not Ask Those Snatched From Death

World, do not ask those snatched from death
where they are going,
they are always going to their graves.
The pavements of the foreign city
were not laid for the music of fugitive footsteps—
The windows of the houses that reflect a lifetime
of shifting tables heaped with gifts from a picture-book
heaven—
were not cut for eyes
which drank terror at its source.
World, a strong iron has cauterized the wrinkle of their smile;
they would like to come to you
because of your beauty,
but for the homeless all ways wither
like cut flowers—

But we have found a friend
in exile: the evening sun.
Blessed by its suffering light
we are bidden to come to it with our sorrow
which walks beside us:
A psalm of night.

—NELLY SACHS

THE ART OF THE FUGUE:
A PRAYER

Radiant silence in Fiesole
And the long climb up a hill which is only one feather
Of the sky, and to set out within the sky,
As the dark happy Florentine would surely gather
All that he had to gather and every night set forth
And enter the pearl.

Florence below our hands, the city that yielded
Up the last secret of Hell.
Fiesole below me and around me and the wings
Of the invisible musician Brother Esposito folded
Around me and my girl.

And the organ
Silent in its longing for the only love.
And Bach and Dante meeting and praying
Before the music began.

And a little bell ringing halfway down the hill.

And me there a long way from the cold dream of Hell.
Me, there, alone, at last,
At last with the dust of my dust,
As far away as I will ever get from dying,
And the two great poets of God in the silence
Meeting together.

And Esposito the organist waiting to begin.
And the little bell halfway down delicately drifting off.

And Florence down there darkening, waiting to begin.

And me there alone at last with my only love,
Waiting to begin.

Whoever you are, ambling past my grave,
My name worn thin as the shawl of the lovely hill town
Fiesole, the radiance and silence of the sky,
Listen to me:

Though love can be scarcely imaginable Hell,
By God, it is not a lie.

—JAMES WRIGHT

CONTENTMENT IS A SLEEPY THING

Contentment is a sleepy thing!
        If it in death alone must die;
A quiet mind is worse than poverty!
        Unless it from enjoyment spring!
That's blessedness alone that makes a king!
Wherein the joys and treasures are so great,
They all the powers of the soul employ,
        And fill it with a work complete,
        While it doth all enjoy.
True joys alone contentment do inspire,
Enrich content, and make our courage higher.
        Content alone's a dead and silent stone:
        The real life of bliss
        Is glory reigning in a throne,
        Where all enjoyment is
The soul of man is so inclin'd to see,
Without his treasures no man's soul can be,
        Nor rest content uncrown'd!
        Desire and love
Must in the height of all their rapture move,
        Where there is true felicity.

—THOMAS TRAHERNE

$\mathcal{S}$OMETIMES A MAN STANDS UP

Sometimes a man stands up during supper
and walks outdoors, and keeps on walking,
because of a church that stands somewhere in the East.

And his children say blessings on him as if he were dead.

And another man, who remains inside his own house,
stays there, inside the dishes and in the glasses,
so that his children have to go far out into the world
toward that same church, which he forgot.

—RAINER MARIA RILKE

$\mathcal{T}$HE SEVEN STAGES

My soul grieved seven times: the first time when it tried to attain
dignity by way of lowliness; the second when it limped before the
crippled; the third when it was given a choice between the easy
path and the rough one and chose the former; the fourth when it
transgressed and consoled itself with the transgressions of others;
the fifth when it feigned patience, despite its weakness, and
attributed its endurance to strength; the sixth when it lifted its
train from the mud of life; and the seventh when it chanted
hymns before the Almighty and believed its chanting an innate
virtue.

—GIBRAN KAHLIL GIBRAN

4 2

In this river the heart is like a ruined waterwheel; in whichever direction it turns, there is water before it;

And even if you turn your back to the water, the water runs hurrying before you.

How shall the shadow save its soul from the sun, seeing that its soul is in the hand of the sun?

If the shadow stretches forth its neck, the sun's face that instant is shrouded.

Brave Sun, before which this sun in heaven quivers with fear like quicksilver!

The moon is like quicksilver on a palsied palm—one night only, and for the rest it is poured forth;

In every thirty nights, two nights it is united and lean, for the rest it endures separation, and separation is torture.

Though it is wretched, it is fresh of face; laughter is the habit and wont of lovers.

It lives laughing, and likewise dies laughing, for its return is to laughing fortune.

Keep silent, for the faults of vision always come from question and answer.

—RUMI

$\mathcal{T}$HE BLESSING ATTRIBUTED TO SAINT CLARE

May the Lord bless you and keep you.
May He show His face to you and be merciful to you.
May He turn His countenance to you and give you peace.

I, Clare, a handmaid of Christ, a little plant of our holy Father
Francis, a sister and mother of you and the other Poor Sisters,
although unworthy, ask our Lord Jesus Christ through His
mercy and through the intercession of His most holy Mother
Mary, of Blessed Michael the Archangel and all the holy angels
of God, and of all His men and women saints, that the heavenly
Father give you and confirm for you this most holy blessing in
heaven and on earth.

I bless you in my life and after my death as much as I can and
more than I can with all the blessings with which the Father of
mercies has and will have blessed His sons and daughters in
heaven and on earth.

Always be lovers of God and your souls and the souls of your
Sisters, and always be eager to observe what you have promised
the Lord.

May the Lord be with you always and, wherever you are, may
you be with Him always. Amen.

—CLARE OF ASSISI

Come pass me the cup quickly and hand it on;
Love first appeared easy, but trouble fell on me.
The wind discloses the musk of your hair;
My heart was twisted in that musky flame.
In my love's house, there is no peace in pleasure.
At every breath, the caravan bells cry: ride on.
Stain your prayer-rug with wine if the wise man tells you,
For that traveler knows the road's news
And the customs of its houses.
Waves, black night, and the whirlpool are my terrors.
Where do the carefree careless know me?
Their life is on the shore. All my work
Has been drawn from self-interest to infamy.
How can I conceal what they would celebrate?
Hafez, do not give up what you desire,
For what you love, leave the world, forsake it.

—HAFEZ

$\mathcal{T}$HE LIANA

In the secret of night
my prayer climbs like the liana,
gropes like a blind man,
sees more than the owl.

Up the stalk of night
that you loved, that I love,
creeps my torn prayer,
rent and mended, uncertain and sure.

Here the path breaks it,
here breezes lift it,
wind flurries toss it,
and something I don't know
hurls it to earth again.

Now it creeps like the liana,
now geysers up, at every thrust
received and returned.

My prayer is, and I am not.
It grows, and I perish.
I have only my hard breath,
my reason and my madness.
I cling to the vine of my prayer.
I tend it at the root
of the stalk of night.

Always the same glory
of life, the same death.
you who hear me and I who see you,
and the vine that tenses, snaps, recoils,
lacerates my flesh.

Grasp the weakening tip
when my prayer reaches you
so that I may know you have it;
sustain it the long night.

Of an instant night hardens,
hard as ipecac, as eucalyptus:
becomes black stretch of road
and frozen hush of river.
My liana climbs and climbs
till tendrils touch your side.

When the vine breaks, you raise it,
and by your touch I know you.
Then my breath abates,
my ardor and my message.
I grow still. I name you. One by one
I tell you all your names.
The liana caresses your throat,
binds you fast, entwines you, and rests.

My poor breath quickens
and words become flood.
My prayer, moored, at last
grows quiet, at last is still.

Then I know the dark vine
of my blood is anchored,
the broken skein of my body
unraveled in prayer;
and I learn that the patient
cry, broken, mends;
climbs again and climbing,
the more it suffers, the more attains.

Gather up my prayer tonight.
Take it and hold it.
Sleep, my love, let my sleep
fall to me in prayer,
and as we were on earth,
so let us remain.

—GABRIELA MISTRAL

Near the wall of a house painted
to look like stone,
I saw visions of God.

A sleepless night that gives others a headache
gave me flowers
opening beautifully inside my brain.

And he who was lost like a dog
will be found like a human being
and brought back home again.

Love is not the last room: there are others
after it, the whole length of the corridor
that has no end.

—YEHUDA AMICHAI

$\mathscr{B}$IOGRAPHICAL NOTES

YEHUDA AMICHAI (1924–) is an Israeli poet born in Wurzburg, Germany. He emigrated to Palestine in 1935. Amichai's books have been translated into many languages. English translations of his collections of poetry include *Amen, Travels of a Latter Day Benjamin of Tudela,* and *Time.*

KWAJA ABDULLAH ANSARI (1006–1089) was a major writer of early Persian mystical literature. His best known work is *Intimate Conversations,* a literary work which has been used traditionally as a devotional text.

'ATTAR (1120–1220), born Farid ud-Din Attar, was a twelfth century mystic. The title 'Attar signifies his position as a pharmacist/perfumist. The word has come into English usage (for example, Emily Dickinson's "Attar from the Rose," poem #675). *The Conference of the Birds* remains a classic Sufi allegory depicting the soul's quest for unity with the Divine. Later in his life, 'Attar was tried for heresy and banished from his home in Nishapur, India.

W.H. AUDEN (1907–1973), poet, critic, translator, and editor, was born in York, England. He moved to the United States in 1939 and became a citizen in 1946. Associated with the group of writers—Christopher Isherwood, Stephen Spender, Louis MacNiece—who came of age between World Wars I and II, Auden was a dominant figure in twentieth century British and American literature. He was awarded a King's Gold Medal for Poetry (1937), a Pulitzer Prize in Poetry (1948) for *The Age of Anxiety*, and a National Book Award (1956) for *The Shield of Achilles*.

CHARLES BAXTER (1947–), a fiction writer and poet, is Professor of English at the University of Michigan, Ann Arbor. He won the AWP Award Series in Short Fiction (1984) for *Harmony of the World*. His other books include *Through the Safety Net* (1985) and *Shadow Play* (a novel, 1993).

WILLIAM BLAKE (1757–1827) was an English poet, printer, and mystic. His poetry often reflects his mistrust of materialism and rationalism and his belief in the spiritual truths of the imagination. With the assistance of his wife, Catherine Boucher, Blake printed three books of his own poetry: *Poetical Sketches* (1783), *Songs of Innocence* (1789), and *Songs of Experience* (1794).

PAUL CELAN (1920–1970) was born in Romania to a Jewish family (as Paul Ancel or Antschel. "Celan" is an anagram he adopted in 1946 when his poems first appeared). He managed to escape the Nazi deportation in 1942 but remained in a Romanian labor camp until the liberation. His parents perished in an extermination camp. After finishing his studies, he moved to Vienna and finally, in 1948, to Paris, where he died in 1970, a suicide.

CLARE OF ASSISI (1193–1253), friend and follower of Saint Francis, founded the order of nuns referred to as the Poor Clares. Clare was canonized a saint in 1255. She is recognized as one of the great figures of early Renaissance church history.

JOHN CLARE (1793–1864), a farm laborer in his native Northamptonshire, was celebrated for a time as the "peasant poet." Later, he fell into obscurity and poverty. He suffered from mental illness and eventually was committed to Northampton General Lunatic Asylum in 1841, where he lived until his death, continuing to write poetry. He is one of the great lyrical nature poets in English.

LUCILLE CLIFTON (1936–) is a poet and professor of literature and creative writing at the University of California, Santa Cruz. Clifton won a Juniper Prize in 1980. Her books include *Earth: New Poems* (1987), *An Ordinary Woman* (1974), and *Next: New Poems* (1987).

PADRAIG DALY (1943–) is a priest living and working in Dublin. His books include *A Celibate Affair* and *Nowhere but in Praise*.

MICHEL DEGUY (1930–) is a poet, translator, and lecturer in French at the University of Paris. In addition to his work on Thomas Mann, Deguy has published several volumes of poetry. His most recent collections are *Figurations* (1969), *Tombeau de du Bellay* (1973), and *Donnant Donnant* (1981).

EMILY DICKINSON (1830–1886) is one of America's most beloved and most widely known poets. In her home in Amherst, Massachusetts, Dickinson lived a rich life of seclusion and contemplation. None of her poems was published in her lifetime.

BLAGA DIMITROVA has published several volumes of poetry: *Gong* (1976), *Prostranstra* (1980), and *Labirint* (1987). A collection of her poems entitled *Because the Sea Is Black* (1989) is available in English translation.

JOHN DONNE (1572–1631) was a poet, Anglican divine, and the dean of St. Paul's in London. He wrote his most well-known work, the "Holy Sonnets," around 1607. Although Donne ultimately rejected the Catholic faith he was raised in, his thinking was affected profoundly by his early Catholicism. In the 1590s he studied law at the Inns of Court in London; this legal training shows in the rigorous arguments put forth in his sonnets.

LOUISE ERDRICH (1954–) is a poet and fiction writer of Chippewa and German-American descent. Her books include *Jacklight* (1984), *The Beet Queen* (1986), *Tracks* (1988), *Baptism of Desire* (1989), *Love Medicine* (1984), and *The Bingo Palace* (1994).

PADRIAC FALLON (1905–1974) was born in Athenry, County Galway, and wrote stories, articles, and radio plays. His published books of poetry include *Poems and Versions* and *Poems*.

FRANCIS OF ASSISI (ca. 1181–1226) founded the Franciscan order and is the principal patron saint of Italy. Born of a wealthy cloth merchant, Francis renounced his material possessions and his family in order to assume a life of poverty. The early rule of the Franciscan order was a simple rule of life: "To follow the teachings of our Lord Jesus Christ and to walk in his footsteps."

GIBRAN KAHLIL GIBRAN (1883–1931), born in poverty in Lebanon, emigrated to America and returned to Lebanon to study Arabic literature. He wrote in Arabic and English and is best known in the United States for his extremely popular book, *The Prophet*. His influence in Arabic literature in this century has been immense, especially through his prose poetry.

ALLEN GINSBERG (1926–) is well known for *Howl and Other Poems* (1956), one of the most widely translated books in the twentieth century. Ginsberg is the cofounder and director emeritas of the Naropa Institute. He published his *Collected Poems* in 1984.

LOUISE GLÜCK (1943–) is a poet and senior lecturer in English at Williams College. Her most recent volumes of poetry are *Ararat* (1990) and *The Wild Iris* (1992), for which she won a Pulitzer Prize.

LINDA GREGG (1942–) is a poet whose books include *Too Bright to See* (1981), *Eight Poems* (1983), and *Scent of White* (1984). She has taught at Syracuse University and the University of Iowa.

HAFEZ (1320–1391), literally "one who knows the Koran by heart," was the pen name of Shadsuddin Mohammad of Shiraz. Hafez was both a religious scholar and courtier. Similarly, his poems temper mysticism with a love of wine, roses, nightingales, and friends. Hafez is widely held to be Iran's greatest lyric poet and master of the *ghazal* form. Ralph Waldo Emerson considered Hafez and Shakespeare to be the two examples of "pure poets."

'AYN AL-QOZAT HAMADANI (1098–1132) is celebrated for his subtle poetic descriptions and interpretations of mystical Sufi states. Hamadani was charged with heresy by the orthodox religious establishment and executed in Baghdad at the age of thirty-three.

GEORGE HERBERT (1593–1633), along with Donne, Vaughan, and several others, was one of the English "metaphysical poets" of the seventeenth century. Herbert was born to a distinguished family, and for a time considered a life at the Court of James I. He took Holy Orders in the Anglican Church, however, and spent the last three years of his life as pastor of a small, impoverished parish near Salisbury.

EDWARD HIRSCH (1950–) has published four books of poems: *For the Sleepwalkers* (1981), *Wild Gratitude* (1986), which won the National

Book Critics' Circle Award, *The Night Parade* (1989), and *Earthy Measures* (1994). He teaches at the University of Houston.

GERARD MANLEY HOPKINS (1844–1889) was raised in a staunch Anglican family, but he converted to Catholicism and was ordained a Jesuit priest in 1877. He preached in Liverpool and served as Professor of Greek at Catholic University in Dublin. Known as a great technical innovator, Hopkins has also been credited with having transformed poetry into a devotional medium.

JOHN OF THE CROSS (1542–1591) was a Spanish Carmelite mystic and poet who wrote in the tradition that cast the poet in the role of spiritual seer. His work resembles the poetry of the medieval Spanish troubadours insofar as it embraces the spiritual truth that all love is a reflection of the love of God. His work also upholds many notions that are Sufi in origin, attesting to the presence of Islamic culture and the diverse spiritual climate of Spain at the time in which he wrote.

THOMAS KINSELLA (1928–) was born in Dublin. Special editions of his work have been published by the Peppercannister Press. His books include *Moralities, Another September, Downstream,* and *Nightwalker and Other Poems.*

ELSE LASKER-SCHULER (1869–1945) was born to a bourgeois Jewish family in Elberfeld, Germany, and moved to Berlin in 1894 at the time of her first marriage. There, her only child, Paul, was born in 1899. She divorced, and entered the artistic and bohemian life of the city. "I'm not a human being," she once said. "I'm weather." Her son died before he was thirty, and the politics of the Third Reich sent her into exile, eventually to Palestine, where she lived out her last years.

PHILLIS LEVIN (1954–) is the author of *Temples and Fields* (1988), which won the Poetry Society of America's First Book Award. She is a professor in the MFA program at the University of Maryland, and Senior Editor of *Boulevard* magazine. Her second book of poems, *The Afterimage*, is forthcoming from Copper Beech Press.

NAZIK AL-MALA'IKA (1923–) is a poet and critic who was born in Baghdad to a literary family. She attended a teachers college there, later studied English literature at Princeton, and has taught at various universities in Iraq and Kuwait. She has been a key figure in the free verse movement in Iraqi poetry. She has published two collections of poetry, *Ashes and Shrapnel* (1949) and *The Trough of the Wave* (1958).

OSIP MANDELSTAM (ca. 1891–1938), a Russian poet, novelist, essayist, and critic, was arrested in 1934 for reading an anti-Stalin poem. With the help of his friend Boris Pasternak, Mandelstam was released from prison in 1937, but he was imprisoned again later that year. Mandelstam wrote a collection of autobiographical essays and several volumes of poetry. He is acknowledged, along with Pasternak, Anna Ahkmatova, and Marina Tsvetaeva, as one of the greatest Russian poets of the twentieth century.

LINDA MCCARRISTON (1943–) has published two collections of poems, *Talking Soft Dutch* (1984) and *Eva-Mary*, which was a National Book Award finalist in 1991. She teaches at the University of Alaska, Anchorage.

THOMAS MERTON (1915–1968) was a Cistercian monk, essayist, poet, and spiritual writer. Merton's translations of Chaung Tzu are Merton creations inspired by translations of Chaung's work. Chaung Tzu was a Chinese philosopher, poet and chief spokesman for Taoism and its founder (Lao Tzu).

CZESLAW MILOSZ (1911–) was born in Lithuania, raised in Poland, and has lived in the United States since 1960. Milosz is a poet, critic, essayist, novelist, translator, and Professor Emeritus at the University of California, Berkeley. He was awarded the Nobel Prize for Literature (1980).

GABRIELA MISTRAL (1890–1957) was a Chilean poet and the first Latin American to be awarded a Nobel Prize for Literature (1945). In addition to her literary distinction, she led an active international life as an educator. She was a delegate to the United Nations and played an important part in the founding of UNICEF. She spent the last years of her life in New York.

JOHN MONTAGUE (1929–) was born in New York but has lived most of his life in Ireland, where he was raised by two aunts on a farm in Garvaghey. Montague's most recent volumes of poetry are *A Slow Dance* (1975), *O Rida's Farewell* (1975), and *The Great Cloak* (1978). He is also an editor and translator of the *Faber Book of Irish Verse* (1972).

PAUL MURRAY (1947–) is a Dominican priest. He teaches at the Dominican Studium in Tallaght, County Dublin.

ORKHAN MUYASSAR (1914–1965) was a Syrian poet and critic, born in Istanbul. He was highly cultivated and fluent in several languages, including English (he lived for a time in Chicago). He was much interested in surrealism. Author of three books of criticism, Muyassar was instrumental in bringing European surrealism to Syrian literature.

HUDA NA'MANI (1930–) is a Syrian poet who has studied law, literature, Sufism, and Islamic studies. She has written several volumes, of which the most recent are *Love Poems* (1973) and *I Remember I Was a Dot, I Was a Circle* (1978).

AMJAD NASIR (1955–) is a young Jordanian poet who has worked in television and print journalism. He is one of the most active of the young generation of Arabic poets. His latest collection of poetry is *Shepherds of Solitude* (1986).

GHARIB NAWAZ (1143–1236) was head of a Sufi order. He was eventually sent by his master to India, where he gained a large following. When Nawaz died, an exquisite shrine, known as the Mecca of India, was erected in Ajmer. In his poems Nawaz often refers to himself as "Mo'in."

MARY OLIVER (1935–) has written several books of poetry, including *Twelve Moons* (1978) and *American Primitive* (1983), for which she was awarded a Pulitzer Prize.

SYLVIA PLATH (1932–1963) has been linked with Anne Sexton and Robert Lowell as a member of the confessional movement in American poetry. Plath's books include *The Colossus and Other Poems* (1962), *Ariel* (1965), and *Collected Poems*, which was awarded a Pulitzer Prize.

KATHLEEN RAINE (1908–) is a poet, memorist, critic, translator, and lecturer at Morely College in London. Raine's poetry is often associated with the Romantic tradition and with William Blake in particular. Her collections of poetry include *Stone and Flower* (1943), *Living in Time* (1946), and *Collected Poems* (1956).

MELECH RAVITCH (1893–1976) moved to Vienna after World War I, where he was influenced by German Expressionism. He moved to Montreal in 1941. His volumes of poetry include *Song of My Songs* (1954) and *The Main Thing . . . I Forgot* (1969).

CHARLES REZNIKOFF (1894–1976) studied journalism and law before devoting himself to writing. He wrote prose and drama, but is better known for his poetry, which has been published by Black Sparrow Press.

Fu'AD RIFQA (1930–) is a Lebanese poet, scholar, and a professor of philosophy at Beirut University College. His books include *Anchor on the Bay* (1961) and *Poetry and Death* (1973).

RAINER MARIA RILKE (1875–1926), a German-language poet, was born in Prague and moved to Paris in 1902. Under the tutelage of Rodin, he wrote *The Book of Pictures* (1902–1906). As a young poet, Rilke aspired to writing a new kind of poetry about *things* as opposed to feelings, yet he was also deeply moved by the German expressionists. He is best known for his *Elegies*, which took him over ten years to complete, and his fifty-four *Sonnets to Orpheus*, which he wrote in a moment of inspired creation in 1922.

[MAWLANA JALALODDIN] RUMI (1207–1273) is the best known of Persian mystic poets to Western readers. The body of work he left is staggering: his lengthy mediation upon religious mysticism, the *Mathnavi*, is composed of more than 26,000 verses. In addition, he composed 30,000 lyric poems, many of which were said to have come to him while he was in a trance.

NELLY SACHS (1891–1970) was a German poet, playwright, and translator. Sachs's family eluded the Nazis by immigrating to Sweden in 1940. Much of Sachs's poetry attests to the suffering of the Jews, and it also draws its inspiration from Jewish and Christian mysticism. Sachs ranks with Else Lasker-Schuler as the foremost poets of the German language in this century. In 1966 she was awarded a Nobel Prize for Literature.

SANA'I (d. 1131) was one of the first great Sufi poets of Iran. He began his career as a court poet, then turned to mystical verse after a spiritual conversion. Sana'i adapted the traditional poetic forms of the epic *(mathnawi)* and the love lyric *(ghazal)* to didactic and mystical purpose. He is also remembered as the spiritual teacher of Rumi.

VICTOR SEGALEN (1878–1919) was a French poet and physician. While stationed with the French navy in Tahiti, Segalen studied Gauguin's manuscripts and published the prose work *Les Immemoriaux*. From 1909 to 1914 he lived in China, where he was a professor of medicine. With the exception of *Steles* (1912), most of Segalen's poetry was published posthumously: *Steles, Pientures, Equipée* (1955) and *Ode, Suivi de Thibet* (1963).

AHMAD SHAUQI (1869–1932) was an Egyptian and an highly influential figure in Arabic poetry during the first third of this century. His popularity was so widespread among the general public that he was named "Prince of Poets" at the pan-Arab celebrations in Egypt (1927). His collected poems are available in two volumes under the title *Diwan Ahmad Shauqi*.

CHRISTOPHER SMART (1722–1771) is most widely known for his epigrams, his occasional poetry, and his "A Song to Daniel," which was printed in 1763. He was admitted twice to Bethlehem Hospital for insanity—for his disconcerting habit of praying without ceasing.

GERALD STERN (1925–) is a poet and professor of English at the University of Iowa. His recent volumes of poetry include *Lovesick* (1988) and *New and Selected Poems* (1989).

WALLACE STEVENS (1879–1955) was a poet and vice-president of the Hartford Accident and Indemnity Co. Along with T.S. Eliot and William Carlos Williams, Stevens is one of the most influential American poets of the age. His works include *Ideas of Order* (1936), *The Man With the Blue Guitar* (1937) and *Parts of a World* (1942).

JULES SUPERVIELLE (1884–1960) was born in Montevideo, Uruguay, and went to France at age ten, where he was educated. He divided his time between the two countries. Rilke, whom he met in 1923, was a strong influence on his work. Besides poetry, he wrote novels, stories, and plays. New Directions published an English translation of his work in 1967 titled *Selected Writings*.

ABRAHAM SUTZKEVER (1913–) was born in Vilna. He eluded the Nazis by immigrating to Russia. He is the editor of the Yiddish literary magazine *Goldene Keit*. He lives in Israel.

ALFRED TENNYSON (1809–1892) was poet laureate of England. His most well-known works are *The Charge of the Light Brigade* (1854) and *The Idylls of the King* (1859), a poem on the Arthurian legend.

THOMAS TRAHERNE (1637–1674), English poet and chaplain, is known for his prose meditations and metaphysical poetry.

MARINA TSVETAEVA (1892–1941) was born in Moscow to an artistic family. She was recognized as an important poet with her first book while still in her teens. She was caught up in the desperate postrevolutionary period in the Soviet Union and later as an emigré in Prague and Paris. She returned to the Soviet Union, where she suffered grinding poverty, and eventually committed suicide in 1941. Along with Mandelstam, Pasternak, and Akhmatova, she is held as one of the greatest poets of the century.

FADWA TUQAN (1917–) was raised in Nablus, Palestine. Since the June 1967 war, in which her hometown fell to Israel, resistance has been a primary theme in her work. Her most recent collections of poetry are *Horsemen and the Night* (1969) and *Alone on the Summit of the World* (1973).

AHMAD AL-MUSHARI AL-'UDWANI (1923–) is a Kuwaiti poet who received a traditional Islamic education in Cairo. He went on to an administrative career in various cultural posts. His poetry reveals the struggle between his skeptical intelligence and his Islamic formation. He has published a volume of poetry called *Wings of the Storm* (1980).

HENRY VAUGHAN (1622–1695) wrote poetry and practiced medicine. Vaughan received some recognition in his lifetime for his "Silex Scintillans," a collection of sacred poetry, but his poetry remained relatively obscure until it was rediscovered by Wordsworth in the late eighteenth century.

JAMES WRIGHT (1927–1980) was a poet, translator, and a professor of English at Barnard. Among his many awards and fellowships, Wright won the Yale Series of Younger Poets Award (1957) for *The Green Wall* and a Pulitzer Prize in Poetry (1972) for his *Collected Poems*.

WILLIAM BUTLER YEATS (1865–1939) was born in Dublin. Along with Ezra Pound and T.S. Eliot, Yeats is a poet whose name is synonomous with modernism. Among his many achievements, Yeats founded the Abbey Theatre, and he was awarded the Nobel Prize for Literature.

TRANSLATION CREDITS

YEHUDA AMICHAI
"The Course of a Life," "Near the Wall of a House," "Psalm," trans. Chana Bloch; "And That Is Your Glory," trans. Stephen Mitchell. From *The Selected Poetry of Yehuda Amichai*, edited and newly translated by Chana Bloch and Stephen Mitchell (New York: Harper & Row, 1986).

KWAJA ABDULLAH ANSARI
From "Intimate Conversations with God," trans. Wheeler M. Thackston. From Ibn 'Ata' Illah *The Book of Wisdom/Kwaja Abdullah Ansari* trans. *Intimate Conversations* (New York: Paulist Press, 1978).

'ATTAR
"Invocation," trans. by C. S. Nott (London 1974). From *The Drunken Universe: An Anthology of Persian Sufi Poetry*, translated and compiled by Peter Lamborn Wilson and Nasrollah Pourjavady (Grand Rapids: Phanes Press, 1987).

PAUL CELAN
"Zurich, The Stork Inn," "Into the Foghorn," "Psalm," "Thread Suns,"
trans. Michael Hamburger. From *Paul Celan: Poems*, selected, translated,
and introduced by Michael Hamburger (New York: Persea Books,
1952).

CHUANG TZU
"The Breath of Nature," trans. Thomas Merton. From *The Way of
Chuang Tzu* (New York: New Directions, 1965).

CLARE OF ASSISI
"The Blessing Attributed to Saint Clare," trans. Regis J. Armstrong
O.F.M., Cap., and Ignatius C. Brady O.F.M. From *Francis and Clare:
The Complete Works* (New York: Paulist Press, 1982).

MICHEL DEGUY
"When the wind . . . ," trans. Clayton Eshleman. From *The Random
House Book of Twentieth-Century French Poetry*, edited by Paul Auster
(New York: Random House, 1982).

BLAGA DIMITROVA
"The blind woman was more intimate with it," trans. Niko Boris and
Heather McHugh. From *Because the Sea Is Black*, Wesleyan University
Press.

FRANCIS OF ASSISI
"The Canticle of Brother Sun," trans. Regis J. Armstrong O.F.M.,
Cap., and Ignatius C. Brady O.F.M. From *Francis and Clare: The
Complete Works* (New York: Paulist Press, 1982).

GIBRAN KAHLIL GIBRAN
"The Seven Stages," trans. Adnan Haydar and Michael Beard. From
Modern Arabic Poetry, edited by Salma Khadra Jayyusi (New York: Co-
lumbia University Press, 1987).

HAFEZ
"Come pass me the cup . . . ," trans. R.M. Rehder. From *Anthology of Islamic Literature* (Holt, Rhinehart and Winston, 1964).

'AYN AL-QOZAT HAMADANI
"Quatrain," trans. Peter Lamborn Wilson and Nasrollah Pourjavady. From *The Drunken Universe: An Anthology of Persian Sufi Poetry*, translated and compiled by Peter Lamborn Wilson and Nasrollah Pourjavady (Grand Rapids: Phanes Press, 1987).

JOHN OF THE CROSS
"The Dark Night," trans. Kieran Kavanaugh and Otilio Rodriguez. From *The Collected Works of St. John of the Cross* (Washington: ICS Publications, 1979).

ELSE LASKER-SCHULER
All poems translated by Robert P. Newton. From *Your Diamond Dreams Cut Open My Arteries.* (University of North Carolina Press, 1982).

NAZIK AL-MALA'IKA
"Song for the Moon," trans. Matthew Sorenson and Christopher Middleton. From *Modern Arabic Poetry*, edited by Salma Khadra Jayyusi (New York: Columbia University Press, 1987).

OSIP MANDELSTAM
"15," trans. David McDuff. From *Osip Mandelstam: Selected Poems* (New York: Farrar, Straus and Giroux, 1973).

CZESLAW MILOSZ
"On Angels," trans. by the author. From *Czeslaw Milosz: Selected Poems*, revised edition (New York: The Ecco Press, 1978).

GABRIELA MISTRAL
"The Pious One," "Rocking," "The Liana," and "The House," trans. Doris Dana. From *Selected Poems of Gabriela Mistral*, translated and edited by Doris Dana (Johns Hopkins Press, 1972).

ORKHAN MUYASSAR
"Lost," trans. Lena Jayyusi and Samuel Hazo. From *Modern Arabic Poetry*, edited by Salma Khadra Jayyusi (New York: Columbia University Press, 1987).

HUDA NA'MANI
"Love Poem," trans. Lena Jayyusi and Samuel Hazo. From *Modern Arabic Poetry*, edited by Salma Khadra Jayyusi (New York: Columbia University Press, 1987).

AMJAD NASIR
"Loneliness," trans. May Jayyusi and Charles Doria. From *Modern Arabic Poetry*, edited by Salma Khadra Jayyusi (New York: Columbia University Press, 1987).

GHARIB NAWAZ
"Riddle," trans. by Peter Lamborn Wilson and Nasrollah Pourjavady. From *The Drunken Universe: An Anthology of Persian Sufi Poetry*, translated and compiled by Peter Lamborn Wilson and Nasrollah Pourjavady (Grand Rapids: Phanes Press, 1987).

MELECH RAVITCH
"Twelve Lines About the Burning Bush," trans. Ruth Whitman. From *Voices Within the Ark: Modern Jewish Poets*, edited by Howard Schwartz and Anthony Rudolf (New York: Avon Books, 1980).

FU'AD RIFQA
"The Fortune Teller," trans. Sargon Boulus and Samuel Hazo. From *Modern Arabic Poetry*, edited by Salma Khadra Jayyusi (New York: Columbia University Press, 1987).

RAINER MARIA RILKE
"I Have Faith," "Just as the Watchman," "Sometimes a Man Stands Up," and "I Love My Life," trans. Robert Bly from *Selected Poems of*

Rainer Maria Rilke, a translation from the German and commentary by Robert Bly (New York: Harper & Row, 1981). "I find you, Lord in all Things and in all" and "Imaginary Career," trans. Stephen Mitchell from *The Selected Poetry of Rainer Maria Rilke*, edited and translated by Stephen Mitchell (New York: Random House, 1982).

RUMI (MAWLANA JALALLODDIN)
"A Thief in the Night," trans. Peter Lamborn Wilson and Nasrollah Pourjavady. From *The Drunken Universe: An Anthology of Persian Sufi Poetry*, "11," "39," and "42," trans. A. J. Arberry. *Mystical Poems of Rumi 1, First Selection, Poems 1–200*, translated from the Persian by A. J. Arberry. "Answers From the Elements," versions done by John Moyne and Coleman Barks from *Open Secret: Versions of Rumi* (Putney: Threshold Books, 1984).

NELLY SACHS
"If the prophets broke in," "Someone will take this ball," and "World, do not ask," trans. Ruth and Matthew Mead; "Chorus of the Stars," trans. Michael Roloff. From *Nelly Sachs: O the Chimneys: Selected Poems, Including the Verse Play, ELI* (New York: Farrar, Straus and Giroux, 1967).

SANA'I
"Invocation," trans. P.L. Wilson and N. Pourjavady. From *The Drunken Universe: An Anthology of Persian Sufi Poetry*, translated and compiled by Wilson and Pourjavady (Grand Rapids: Phanes Press, 1987).

VICTOR SEGALEN
"Hidden Name," trans. Nathaniel Tarn. From *The Random House Book of Twentieth-Century French Poetry*, edited by Paul Auster (New York: Random House, 1982).

AHMAD SHAUQI
"An Andalusian Exile," trans. M. Mustafa Badawi and John Heath-Stubbs. From *Modern Arabic Poetry*, edited by Salma Khadra Jayyusi (New York: Columbia University Press, 1987).

ABRAHAM SUTZKEVER
"Poems from a Diary," trans. Cynthia Ozick. From *The Penguin Book of Modern Yiddish Verse* (New York: Viking Penguin, 1987).

JULES SUPERVIELLE
"Entangled," trans. James Kirkup. From *The Random House Book of Twentieth-Century French Poetry*, edited by Paul Auster (New York: Random House, 1982).

MARINA TSVETAEVA
"I bless the everyday labor," "I am happy to live correctly and simply," trans. Mary Jane White. From *Starry Sky to Starry Sky: Poems by Mary Jane White with Translations of Marina Tsvetaeva* (Stevens Point, Wisconsin: Holy Cow! Press, 1988).

FADWA TUQAN
"I Found It," trans. Patricia Alanah Byrne with the help of Salma Khadra Jayyusi and Naomi Shihab Nye. From *Modern Arabic Poetry*, edited by Salma Khadra Jayyusi (New York: Columbia University Press, 1987).

AHMAD AL-MUSHARI AL-'UDWANI
From "Signs," trans. Hilary Kilpatrick and Charles Doria. From *Modern Arabic Poetry*, edited by Salma Khadra Jayyusi (New York: Columbia University Press, 1987).

Acknowledgments

Many others—poets and writers, translators and editors, as well as readers—helped gather this collection, and pointed the way along trails unknown to me. I am grateful as well to those who reminded me of well-loved works that I had overlooked precisely because of their familiarity. The most surprising part of my task was rereading some of the standard English and American literary canon, as well as sleuthing in contemporary American poetry for "sacred poems": there proved to be so many in our notoriously secular culture.

Thanks, first, to Mary South, who initially proposed the project, and to my agent Rhoda Weyr, who, as ever, made sense of the fine print. Thanks especially to Joanne Wyckoff, who shepherded the book to completion with keen attention. I am grateful as well to her assistant Andrea Schulz. To Ben Bennani I owe the wise counsel early on to tighten the anthology's focus to the three monotheistic religions of the West. I am indebted, as many readers are, to Stephen Mitchell for his exemplary translations and anthologies, including *The Enlightened Heart*, which inspired this collection. My own thinking about sacred poetry is indebted to David Daiches's superb collection of essays, *God and the Poets*.

Allen Ginsberg offered rich and original suggestions and was characteristically generous. Jim Harris of Prairie Lights Books in Iowa City, Anett Jessop at the University of Minnesota, Philip Bergstrom, living and teaching at the time in Turkey, and Robert Bly helped where I was most in need: the search for works from the Islamic tradition.

Ethna McKiernan of Irish Books and Media in Minneapolis did the same generous service for Celtic poetry. Phebe Hanson offered me, from a little-known source, some of the first poems I knew belonged in the collection. Joan Larkin was especially helpful in suggesting women poets for the anthology. Christine Mack Gordon lavishly shared her library of Jewish and Yiddish poems.

Among others who offered poems and suggestions, I wish to remember the generosity of Clark Blaise; Carol Bly; Carol Conroy; Roland Flint; Matthew Fox and his assistant Marie Devlin; Patricia Goedicke; Pamela Holt; Miriam Levine; Kate Martin, OSC; Sandra McPherson; Alicia Ostriker; Walter Pavlich; William Warner; and Annie Wright.

On the home front, I am grateful to Terence Williams, dearest of readers. For her tireless research and meticulous editorial work on permissions and biographies, Rosemarie Johnstone deserves a page of credit of her own. She has my deepest gratitude, once again.

$\mathscr{P}$ERMISSION ACKNOWLEDGMENTS

Grateful acknowledgment is made to the following for permission to reprint previously published material:

Charles Baxter: "Diptych: Jesus and the Stone" from *Imaginary Paintings and Other Poems* by Charles Baxter. Reprinted by permission of the author.

Beacon Press: "Lilies" from *New and Selected Poems* by Mary Oliver. Copyright © 1992 by Mary Oliver. Reprinted by permission of Beacon Press.

BOA Editions, Ltd.: "mary" by Lucille Clifton reprinted from *Good Woman: Poems and a Memoir 1969–1980* by Lucille Clifton. Copyright © 1987 by Lucille Clifton. Reprinted by permission of BOA Editions, Ltd., 92 Park Avenue, Brockport, NY 14420.

Georges Borchardt, Inc.: "15" from *Osip Mandelstam: Selected Poems* by Osip Mandelstam. Copyright © 1973, 1975 by Rivers Press Ltd. Reprinted by permission of Georges Borchardt, Inc.

Curtis Brown Group Ltd.: "God looks on nature with a glorious eye," "Autumn," and "Lord hear my prayer when trouble glooms" from *John Clare* (The Oxford Authors), edited by Eric Robinson and David Powell (Oxford University Press, 1984). Copyright © Eric Robinson 1984. Reprinted by permission of Curtis Brown Group Ltd., London.

Columbia University Press: "The Seven Stages," "Loneliness," "Song for the Moon," "The Fortune Teller," "An Andalusian Exile," "I Found It," "Signs," "Lost," and "Love Poem" from *Modern Arabic Poetry* translated by Salma Khadra Jayyusi. Copyright © 1987 by Columbia University Press. Reprinted by permission of the publisher.

Doris Dana: "The House," "The Pious One," "Rocking," and "The Liana" from *Selected Poems of Gabriela Mistral,* translated by Doris Dana. Copyright © 1972 by Doris Dana. Reprinted by arrangement with Doris Dana, c/o Joan Daves Agency as agent for the proprietor.

Dedalus Press Dublin: "Problem" by Padraig G. Daly from *Poems: Selected and New* (1988).

Ecco Press: "On Angels" from *The Collected Poems 1931–1987* by Czeslaw Milosz. Copyright © 1988 by Czeslaw Milosz Royalties, Inc. First published by The Ecco Press in 1988. "Celestial Music" from *Ararat* by Louise Glück. Copyright © 1990 by Louise Glück. First published by The Ecco Press in 1990. Reprinted by permission.

Clayton Eshleman and Editions Gallimard: "When the Wind" from *Given Giving: Selected Poems of Michel Deguy,* translated from the French by Clayton Eshleman, University of California Press, 1984. "When the Wind" by Michel Deguy originally appeared in *Oui-Dire* by Michel Deguy. Copyright © 1966 by Editions Gallimard.

Farrar, Straus & Giroux, Inc.: "The Art of the Fugue: A Prayer" from *Above the River* by James Wright. Copyright © 1990 by Anne Wright.